SX-Key/Blitz Development System Manual

Version 2.0

PARALLAX

www.parallax.com

WARRANTY

Parallax warrants its products against defects in materials and workmanship for a period of 90 days from receipt of product. If you discover a defect, Parallax will, at its option, repair or replace the merchandise, or refund the purchase price. Before returning the product to Parallax, call for a Return Merchandise Authorization (RMA) number. Write the RMA number on the outside of the box used to return the merchandise to Parallax. Please enclose the following along with the returned merchandise: your name, telephone number, shipping address, and a description of the problem. Parallax will return your product or its replacement using the same shipping method used to ship the product to Parallax.

14-DAY MONEY BACK GUARANTEE

If, within 14 days of having received your product, you find that it does not suit your needs, you may return it for a full refund. Parallax will refund the purchase price of the product, excluding shipping/handling costs. This guarantee is void if the product has been altered or damaged. See the Warranty section above for instructions on returning a product to Parallax.

COPYRIGHTS AND TRADEMARKS

ISBN 1-928982-01-8

DISCLAIMER OF LIABILITY

Parallax, Inc. is not responsible for special, incidental, or consequential damages resulting from any breach of warranty, or under any legal theory, including lost profits, downtime, goodwill, damage to or replacement of equipment or property, or any costs of recovering, reprogramming, or reproducing any data stored in or used with Parallax products. Parallax is also not responsible for any personal damage, including that to life and health, resulting from use of any of our products. You take full responsibility for your SX-Key/Blitz and SX chip application, no matter how life-threatening it may be.

WEB SITE AND DISCUSSION LISTS

The Parallax web site (www.parallax.com) has many downloads, products, customer applications and on-line ordering for the components used in this text. We also maintain several e-mail discussion lists for people interested in using Parallax products. These lists are accessible from www.parallax.com via the Support • Discussion Groups menu. These are the lists that we operate:

- SX Tech – Discussion of programming the SX microcontroller with Parallax assembly language tools and 3rd party BASIC and C compilers. Approximately 600 members.
- BASIC Stamps – With over 2,500 subscribers, this list is widely utilized by engineers, hobbyists and students who share their BASIC Stamp projects and ask questions.
- Stamps in Class – Created for educators *and* students, this list has 500 subscribers who discuss the use of the Stamps in Class curriculum in their courses. The list provides an opportunity for both students and educators to ask questions and get answers.
- Parallax Educators – This focus group of 100 members consists exclusively of educators and those who contribute to the development of Stamps in Class. Parallax created this group to obtain feedback on our curricula and to provide a forum for educators to develop Teacher's Guides.
- Parallax Translators – Consisting of less than 10 people, the purpose of this list is to provide a conduit between Parallax and those who translate our documentation to languages other than English. Parallax provides editable Word documents to our translating partners and attempts to time the translations to coordinate with our publications.
- Toddler Robot – A customer created this discussion list to discuss applications and programming of the Parallax Toddler robot.
- Javelin Stamp – Discussion of application and design using the Javelin Stamp, a Parallax module that is programmed using a subset of Sun Microsystems' Java® programming language. Approximately 250 members.

This manual is valid with the following software and firmware versions:

IDE:

SXKey.exe software version 2.0

Firmware:

SX-Key rev. F and SX-Blitz rev. A

The information herein will usually apply to newer versions but may not apply to older versions. New software can be obtained free on our web site (www.parallax.com). If you have any questions about what you need to upgrade your product, please contact Parallax.

Welcome

Thank you for purchasing the Parallax SX-Key®/Blitz development system. We have done our best to produce a full-featured, yet easy to use development system for the SX microcontrollers. The result is the SX-Key and the SX-Blitz; very tiny, full-featured development tools with a Windows® 95 and higher versions interface. We hope you will find this system as enjoyable to use as we do.

This manual is written for the SX20/28 chips with a date code of AB9921AA or later, and SX48/52 chips with a date code of AB0001A or later.

Older chips are not supported by this manual or the SX-Key development system.

Table of Contents

1 Introduction to the SX-Key/Blitz Hardware 13
2 Installing the SX-Key/Blitz Software 15
3 Quick Start Introduction 17
3.1 Connecting and Downloading to the SX Tech Board 17
4 The SX-Key/Blitz Interface 19
4.1 Starting the SX-Key/Blitz Software 19
4.1.1 Command Line Switches 19
4.2 The SX Editor 20
4.3 The Menus 21
4.3.1 The File Menu 21
4.3.2 The Edit Menu 22
4.3.3 The Run Menu 23
4.3.4 The Help Menu 25
4.4 The Windows 25
4.4.1 Print Window 25
4.4.2 Find Window 26
4.4.3 Find/Replace Window 26
4.4.4 Goto Line Number Window 27
4.4.5 Configure Window 28
5 The SX-Key Debugger 31
5.1 The Debugger Windows 31
5.1.1 The Registers Window 31
5.1.2 The Debug Window 34
5.1.3 The Watch Window 35
5.1.4 The Code/List File Window 35
5.1.5 Modifying registers during debugging 36
5.1.6 Breakpoints and the Current Instruction 37
5.1.7 Setting the Program Counter 37
6 The Device Window 39
7 The SASM Assembler 43
7.1 The Structure of an SX Assembly Program 44
7.2 Comments 45
7.3 Assembler Directives 45
7.3.1 The EQU and = Directives 47
7.3.2 The BREAK Directive 47
7.3.3 The CASE and NOCASE Directives 47
7.3.4 The DEVICE Directive 48
7.3.5 The DS Directive 51
7.3.6 The DW Directive 51
7.3.7 The END Directive 51
7.3.8 The ERROR Directive 52
7.3.9 The FREQ Directive 52
7.3.10 The __FUSE and __FUSEX Directives 52

Table of Contents

7.3.11 The ID Directive 53
7.3.12 The IF...ELSE...ENDIF Directive 53
7.3.13 The IF{N}DEF...ELSE...ENDIF Directives 54
7.3.14 The INCLUDE Directive 55
7.3.15 The IRC_CAL Directive 56
7.3.16 The LIST Directive 56
7.3.17 The LPAGE Directive 57
7.3.18 The ORG (Origin) Directive 57
7.3.19 The RADIX Directive 58
7.3.20 The REPT Directive 58
7.3.21 The RESET Directive 59
7.3.22 The SPAC Directive 59
7.3.23 The TITLE and STITLE Directives 60
7.3.24 The WATCH Directive 60
7.4 Macros 62
7.4.1 The MACRO Directive 62
7.4.2 The ENDM Directive 63
7.4.3 The EXITM Directive 63
7.4.4 The LOCAL Directive 63
7.4.5 The EXPAND and NOEXPAND Directives 63
7.4.6 Formal Parameters 64
7.4.7 Macro Invocation 65
7.4.8 Actual Values of Parameters 65
7.4.9 Token Pasting 65
7.4.10 Quoting 65
7.4.11 Macro Examples 66
7.4.11.1 Simple Macros with no Parameters 66
7.4.12 Macros with Formal Parameters by Count 67
7.4.13 Macros with Formal Parameters by Name 68
7.5 Symbols 68
7.6 Labels 69
7.7 Expressions 70
7.8 Data Types 72
7.9 The __SASM Pre-Defined Constant 72
7.10 Files created by SASM 73
7.11 SASM Warning and Error Messages 74
7.12 Reserved Words and Symbols 78
8 The Parallax Assembler 79
8.1 The Structure of an SX Assembly Program 79
8.2 Assembler Directives 79
8.2.1 The Device Directive 79
8.3 Symbols 81
8.4 Labels 81
8.5 Expressions 81
8.6 Error Messages 81

8.7 Data Types 83
8.8 Reserved Words and Symbols 84
9 Upgrading Existing Code for SASM 85
10 SX Special Features and Coding Tips 87
10.1 Introduction 87
10.2 Port Configuration and Usage 87
10.2.1 Port Direction 88
10.2.2 Pull-Up Resistors 89
10.2.3 Logic Level 90
10.2.4 Schmitt-Trigger 91
10.2.5 Edge Detection 92
10.2.6 Wakeup (Interrupt) on Edge Detection 93
10.2.7 Comparator 95
10.3 The SX48/52 Multi-Function Timers 96
10.3.1 PWM Mode 97
10.3.2 Software Timer Mode 98
10.3.3 External Event Counter 98
10.3.4 Capture/Compare Mode 98
10.4 All About Interrupts 99
10.4.1 RTCC Rollover Interrupts 100
10.5 Creating Tables 103
10.5.1 Data Tables 103
10.6 Dealing with Code Pages 105
10.6.1 Branching Across Pages 105
10.6.2 Calling Across Pages with Jump Tables 106
11 Appendix A: SX Features 109
11.1 Introduction 109
11.2 CPU Features 109
11.3 Peripheral and I/O Features 109
12 Appendix B: Instruction Set Overview 111
12.1 Introduction 111
12.2 Instruction Set Summary 111
12.3 Single Word Instructions 114
12.4 Multi-Word Instructions 116
12.5 Instruction Set Quick Reference 118
13 Appendix C: SX Instruction Set 121
13.1 Introduction 121
14 Appendix D: The SX Tech Board 145
14.1 SX Tech Board Features 145
14.2 Connecting and Downloading 146
14.3 SX Tech Board Schematic 147
15 Appendix E: SX Data Sheet 149
15.1 Pinout Information and Descriptions 149
15.2 Architecture 150
15.2.1 Instruction Pipeline 151

15.2.2 Read-Modify-Write Considerations 151
15.2.3 Register Map Structure 151
15.2.4 Special Function Registers 153
15.2.5 IND – The Indirect Register ($00) 153
15.2.6 Real Time Clock/Counter, WREG ($01) 153
15.2.7 PC – Program Counter ($02) 153
15.2.8 STATUS Register ($03) 154
15.2.9 The FSR – File Select Register ($04) 155
15.2.10 Direct Addressing 156
15.2.11 Indirect Addressing 160
15.2.12 The Bank Instruction 161
15.2.13 The Jump Instruction 162
15.2.14 Jumping Across Pages 163
15.2.15 The Call Instruction 163
15.2.16 Calling Across Pages 164
15.2.17 Returning from a subroutine 164
15.2.18 The Stack 165
15.2.19 The Push 165
15.2.20 The Pop 166
15.2.21 Stack Overflow 166
15.2.22 Stack Underflow 166
15.2.23 Returns 166
15.3 Port Configuration Registers 167
15.3.1 Port A Registers 167
15.3.1.1 TRIS_A – Data Direction Register 167
15.3.1.2 LVL_A - TTL/CMOS Select Register 167
15.3.1.3 PLP_A – Pull-Up Resistor Enable Register 167
15.3.2 Port B Registers 168
15.3.2.1 TRIS_B – Data Direction Register 168
15.3.2.2 LVL_B - TTL/CMOS Select Register 168
15.3.2.3 PLP_B – Pull-Up Resistor Enable Register 168
15.3.2.4 ST_B – Schmitt-Trigger Enable Register 169
15.3.2.5 WKEN_B – Wake Up Enable Register 169
15.3.2.6 WKED_B – Wake Up Edge Select Register 169
15.3.2.7 WKPND_B – MIWU Pending Register 169
15.3.2.8 CMP_B – Comparator Enable Register 170
15.3.3 Port C Registers 170
15.3.3.1 TRIS_C – Data Direction Register 170
15.3.3.2 LVL_C - TTL/CMOS Select Register 170
15.3.3.3 PLP_C – Pull-Up Resistor Enable Register 171
15.3.3.4 ST_C – Schmitt-Trigger Enable Register 171
15.3.4 Port D and E Registers (SX48/52) 171
15.4 Control registers 171
15.4.1 Mode register (SX20/28) 171
15.4.2 Mode register (SX48/52) 173

15.4.3 Option..174
15.4.4 Fuse Registers..174
15.5 Interrupts..175
15.5.1 Description..175
15.5.2 The Specifics..175
15.5.3 RTCC Interrupt..175
15.5.4 RB0-RB7 Interrupt..176
15.6 Peripherals..176
15.6.1 Oscillator Driver..176
15.6.1.1 LP, XT and HS Mode..176
15.6.1.2 External RC Mode..178
15.6.1.3 Internal RC Mode..179
16 Index..181

Table of Contents

Figures

Figure 1 - Connecting the SX-Key/Blitz 13
Figure 2 - First Time Running Window 16
Figure 3 - Configure Window 16
Figure 4 - SX Tech Board with SX chip inserted 17
Figure 5 - The SX-Key Icon 19
Figure 6 - The SX Editor 20
Figure 7 - The Find Window 26
Figure 8 - The Find/Replace Window 26
Figure 9 - The Goto Line Number Window 27
Figure 10 - The Configure Window 28
Figure 11 - The Debugger Windows 33
Figure 12 - The Device Window 39
Figure 13 - The Watch Window 61
Figure 14 - TTL and CMOS Levels 90
Figure 15 - Schmitt Trigger Characteristics 91
Figure 16 - SX48/52 Multi-Function Timers 97
Figure 17 - The SX Tech Board 145
Figure 18 - SX Tech Board Schematic 147
Figure 19 - SX Pinouts 149
Figure 20 - Instruction Pipeline 151
Figure 21 - SX20/28 Register Map 152
Figure 22 - SX48/52 Register Map 152
Figure 23 - Rotate Right 155
Figure 24 - Rotate Left 155
Figure 25 - Global Register Addressing SX20/28/48/52 (direct) 156
Figure 26 - SX20/28 General Purpose Register Addressing (direct) 157
Figure 27 - SX48/52 General-Purpose Register addressing (direct) 158
Figure 28- SX20/28 Indirect register addressing 160
Figure 29 - SX48/52 Indirect register addressing 161
Figure 30 - The Jump Instruction 162
Figure 31 - Jumping Across Pages 163
Figure 32 - The Call Instruction 164
Figure 33 - Calling Across Pages 164
Figure 34 - The Push 165
Figure 35 - The Pop 166
Figure 36 - Prescaler Division Ratios 174
Figure 37 - SX with External Crystal 176
Figure 38 - SX with External Ceramic Resonator 177
Figure 39 - SX with External System Clock 178
Figure 40 - External RC Mode 178

Tables

Table 1 - Editor Shortcut Keys 21
Table 2 - Debugger Buttons and Shortcut Keys 35
Table 3 – Register Editing Keys 36
Table 4 - SX Clock Options 40
Table 5 - SASM Directives 46
Table 6 - SX20/28 DEVICE Settings 49
Table 7 - SX48/52 DEVICE Settings 50
Table 8 – Comparison Operators 53
Table 9 - LIST Directive Options 57
Table 10 - WATCH Display Formats 60
Table 11 - Unary Operators 71
Table 12 - Binary Operators 71
Table 13 - Data Types 72
Table 14 - SASM Error and Warning Messages 75
Table 15 - SASM Reserved Words 78
Table 16 - Parallax Assembler DEVICE Options 80
Table 17 - Parallax Assembler Error Messages 81
Table 18 - Parallax Assembler Reserved Words 84
Table 19 - Port Configuration Options 87
Table 20 - MODE Register Settings 88
Table 21 - Interrupt Timing 102
Table 22 - SX Instruction Mnemonics 112
Table 23 - SX Single-Word Instructions 114
Table 24 - SX Multi-Word Instructions 116
Table 25 - SX Instruction Set Quick Reference 118
Table 26 - Symbol and Value Operands 121
Table 27 - Flags and Registers 122
Table 28 - Binary Symbols 122
Table 29 - SX Pins 150
Table 30 - Special Function Registers 153
Table 31 - Bank Addresses and FSR Values 159
Table 32 – SX20/28 Mode Register 172
Table 33 - SX48/52 Mode Register 173
Table 34 – External Component Selection for Crystals (Vdd = 5V) 177
Table 35 - Component Selection for Murata Ceramic Resonators (Vdd = 5.0 V) 177

1 Introduction to the SX-Key/Blitz Hardware

The SX-Key/Blitz hardware consists of the programmer unit, a four-pin programming interface and a standard, female serial port connector (DB9). The serial port connector should be plugged into an available standard, straight-through serial cable on an IBM-compatible PC. The four-pin connector on the SX-Key/Blitz board should be connected to four pins (VSS, VDD, OSC2 and OSC1) of the SX chip. Take care to connect it in the right orientation because this connector is not indexed.

Figure 1 - Connecting the SX-Key/Blitz

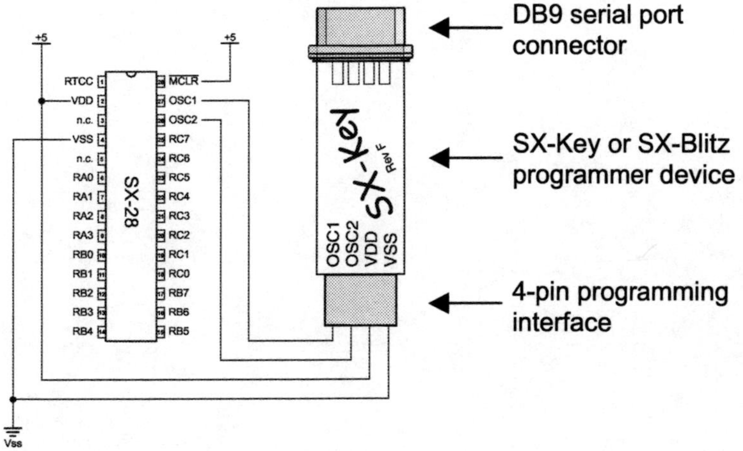

The SX-Key/Blitz is powered by the target circuit's power supply and programming and debugging takes place over the oscillator pins. The power supply to the SX-Key/Blitz must be +5 V DC. If an external crystal, resonator or RC circuit is used, the SX-Key/Blitz can usually remain connected to the SX chip for programming purposes, without affecting the operation of the circuit. When debugging, the SX chip must not have an external clock source since the SX-Key's internal programmable oscillator must be used. ***The SX-Blitz can only program SX chips, it cannot debug them.***

Each SX microcontroller contains the necessary debugger hooks required to perform SX in-circuit debugging. No other supporting chips are necessary for the debugging process. During debugging, the SX-Key provides the oscillator signal to drive the SX microcontroller until such time that a breakpoint is hit or a single step or stop mode is initiated.

Figure 1 - Connecting the SX-Key/Blitz shows all the connections necessary to program, debug and run the SX microcontroller. An external resonator or crystal should be connected to the OSC1 and OSC2 pins to run the SX if the SX-Blitz is used, or if the SX-Key's internal clock oscillator is not used.

1 Introduction the SX-Key/Blitz Hardware

The SX-Blitz is designed to be a lower-cost device for programming the SX chips only (no debugging features are available). The SX-Blitz and SX-Key use the same interface software for programming, however, debugging features will not work with the SX-Blitz.

NOTE: Since the SX-Blitz and SX-Key function almost identically, they will be referred to as the SX-Key / Blitz, except where there are distinct differences.

2 Installing the SX-Key/Blitz Software

Before following the steps in the next chapter, you should first install the SX-Key/Blitz interface on your computer's hard disk.

The SX-Key/Blitz Interface consists of the integrated editor, programmer, and debugger software. The following system requirements are a minimum for using the SX-Key/Blitz Interface:

- 80486 (or higher) IBM or compatible PC;
- Windows 95 or higher operating system;
- 64 Mb of RAM;
- 3 Mb of available hard drive space;
- CD-ROM drive, or access to the Internet;
- 1 available serial port.

To install the SX-Key/Blitz Interface:

1. Insert the Parallax CD-ROM in an available CD-ROM drive.
2. Use the CD's automatic browser to navigate to the Software section.
3. Expand the SX-Key & SX-Blitz folder.
4. Select the 18/28/48/52-pin SX chips (SXKey.exe) item.
5. Click on the Install button.
6. When prompted for the type of installation, select "Typical" in order to have the software installed in the "Programs\Parallax Inc\SX-Key v2.0" folder. Select "Custom" when you want to change the default installation options, like the installation folder.
7. After the setup has finished, you will find a shortcut on the desktop, and a new "Parallax Inc" program group in the Start menu.

You may also download the software from the Parallax web site. There are two different file versions available. One has a size of about 1.2 MB, and the other one of 4.6 MB. When you use the smaller one, it is necessary to have an Internet connection active while installing the software. Select any folder where the downloaded file shall be stored, and then run "Setup_SX-Key_Editor.exe" from this folder.

After you have successfully installed the SX-Key Editor and start it the first time, the dialog shown below opens:

Figure 2 - First Time Running Window

This is to remind you that you should review some basic configuration settings first. Click the OK button, and press Ctrl-U to open the Configuration dialog shown to the right.

The only setting that is important for now is the selection of the serial port to which you have connected the SX-Key/Blitz.

Figure 3 - Configure Window

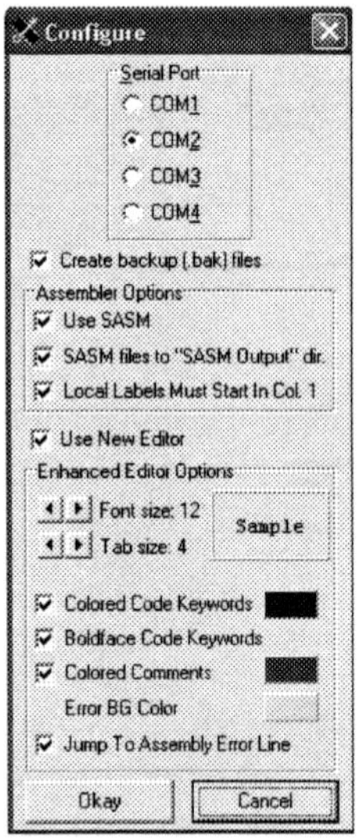

The configuration dialog allows you to select COM1, COM2, COM3, or COM4.

Click the radio button in the "Serial Port" section that matches your installation.

Make sure that the remaining options are set to the defaults as shown here, and then click "Okay" to close the configuration dialog window.

You may keep the SX-Key Editor active because you will need it to perform the next steps below.

3 Quick Start Introduction

This chapter is a quick start guide to connecting the SX-Key/Blitz and programming the SX microcontroller. Without even knowing how the SX-Key/Blitz and the SX chip work, you should be able to obtain satisfactory results from the steps that follow.

3.1 Connecting and Downloading to the SX Tech Board

In order to get familiar with how the SX-Key/Blitz Development System works, we'll use the SX Tech Board to program and run a 28-pin SX chip.

Keep in mind that the SX Tech Board is not a programmer; rather the SX-Key/Blitz is the programmer/debugger device while the SX Tech board is a type of prototyping board. Follow these steps to connect and download a program:

Figure 4 - SX Tech Board with SX chip inserted

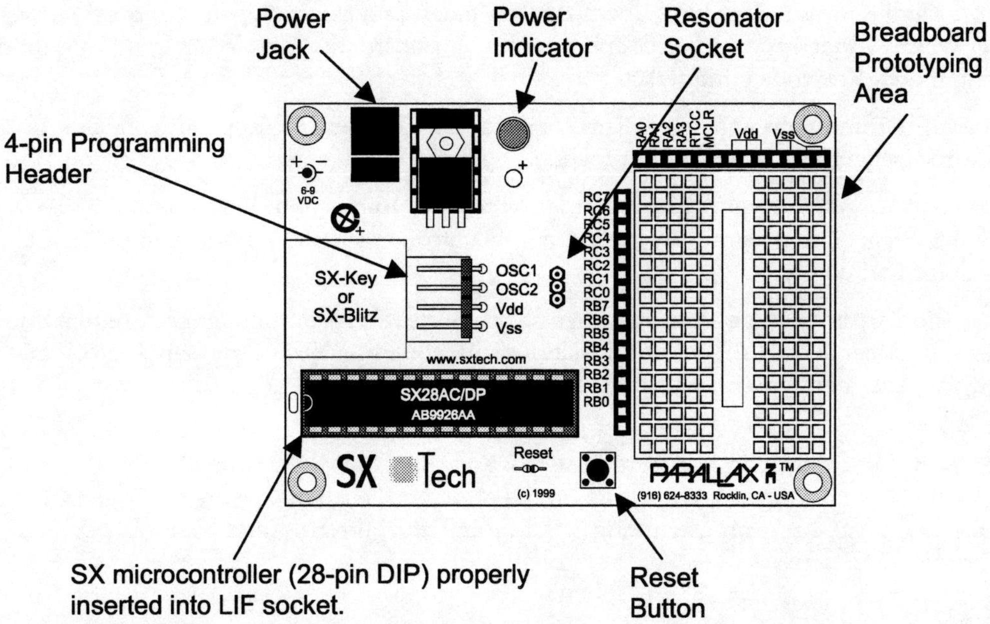

1) Plug an SX28AC/DP into the 28-pin LIF socket on the SX Tech board as shown in Figure 4 - SX Tech Board with SX chip inserted. Make sure it is oriented so that the half-moon notch in the chip faces away from the "Reset" button.

2) Connect the SX-Key/Blitz to a serial cable, and the serial cable to the serial (COM) port on the PC that you have selected in the "Configure" dialog of the SX-Key/Blitz software.

3) Connect the SX-Key/Blitz to the 4-pin programming header with the VSS, VDD, OSC2 and OSC1 indicators lining up with the same indicators on the board Note that the programming header is not indexed. Therefore, double-check the correct orientation of the SX-Key/Blitz.

4) Insert one end of a 470 ohm resister into the RC7 socket (next to the upper left side of the breadboard). Insert the other end of the resister into any hole in the breadboard. See p 147

5) Insert the shorter (Cathode) leg of an LED into the breadboard hole that is closest (horizontally) to the resister leg. Insert the other leg (Anode) of the LED into one of the VDD sockets (next to the top side of the breadboard).

6) Plug the power supply into the SX Tech board and into an available wall outlet. (The power indicator should light up).

7) If it is not still active, start the SX-Key Editor now.

8) In the SX-Key Editor window, pull down the File menu and select "Open" (or press Ctrl-O). In the browser window that appears, select and open the led28.src file. (The led28.src source code should appear in the SX-Key code window).

9) Pull down the Run menu and select Run (or press Ctrl-R). (The SX-Key software should assemble the code and begin the programming process). Assembler error. *

Congratulations! You have just programmed the SX microcontroller with the SX-Key/Blitz Development System. The program in the SX microcontroller should start running. The LED should flash on and off (if wired correctly).

In case you get an error message after you have selected the "Run" option, make sure that you did not modify the source code text in the editor window. If you did, simply re-load the original text by opening it again, and then repeat the steps described above.

Should an error message like "SX-Key not found on COMx" appear, check that you have selected the right serial port for communication with the SX-Key/Blitz, and that the serial cable is correctly connected to the PC, and to the SX-Key/Blitz on the other end. Also make sure that the SX-Key/Blitz is correctly placed on the 4-pin programming header, and that the SX Tech board is powered, i.e. the power indicator LED is active.

* Downloaded SX-Key Software V3.0 6.0MB
" Programming the SX Microcontroller 2nd Source Code ProgSXEdPrei.zip
" SX Source Code Examples.
It worked

4 The SX-Key/Blitz Interface

The SX-Key/Blitz interface is an integrated editor, programmer, and debugger. All the functions of the SX-Key and the SX-Blitz are available through this single software interface.

Throughout the rest of this manual, the SX-Key/Blitz interface will be referred to as the SX editor, or more simply, the editor.

4.1 Starting the SX-Key/Blitz Software

Figure 5 - The SX-Key Icon

During installation, a shortcut was automatically placed on the Windows desktop. Double-click on the SX-Key icon to launch the SX-Key/Blitz interface. In case, the Icon has been deleted from the desktop, you can also start the software via the Windows Start button. Navigate to the Parallax Inc. program group and select "SX-Key v2.0" there.

4.1.1 Command Line Switches

It is also possible to start the SX-Keys software together with parameters from a command line, e.g. using the Windows "Run..." option, or from the DOS command line. The Syntax is:

SxKey /<switch> {/<switch>...} <File name>

When you specify a file name with a ".src" extension, the editor window will open, displaying the contents of the source code file. When you specify an ".sxh" extension instead, the hex file will be opened into the device window.

The /r switch is used to open a file in read-only mode, i.e. it can be displayed but not modified in the editor or in the device window.

For example

SxKey /r test.src

opens the source file named "test", and displays it in the editor window and

SxKey /r test.sxh

opens the hex file named "test", and displays the device window. In both examples, the files are opened read-only, i.e. they cannot be modified.

In addition to the /r switch, the switches /1, /2, /3 and /4 are also defined. They are used to select the COM port where the SX-Key/Blitz is attached. This will override the setting that has been recently made in the Configure window. It is recommended **not** to use these switches; they have been implemented for compatibility reasons only.

4.2 The SX Editor

Figure 6 - The SX Editor

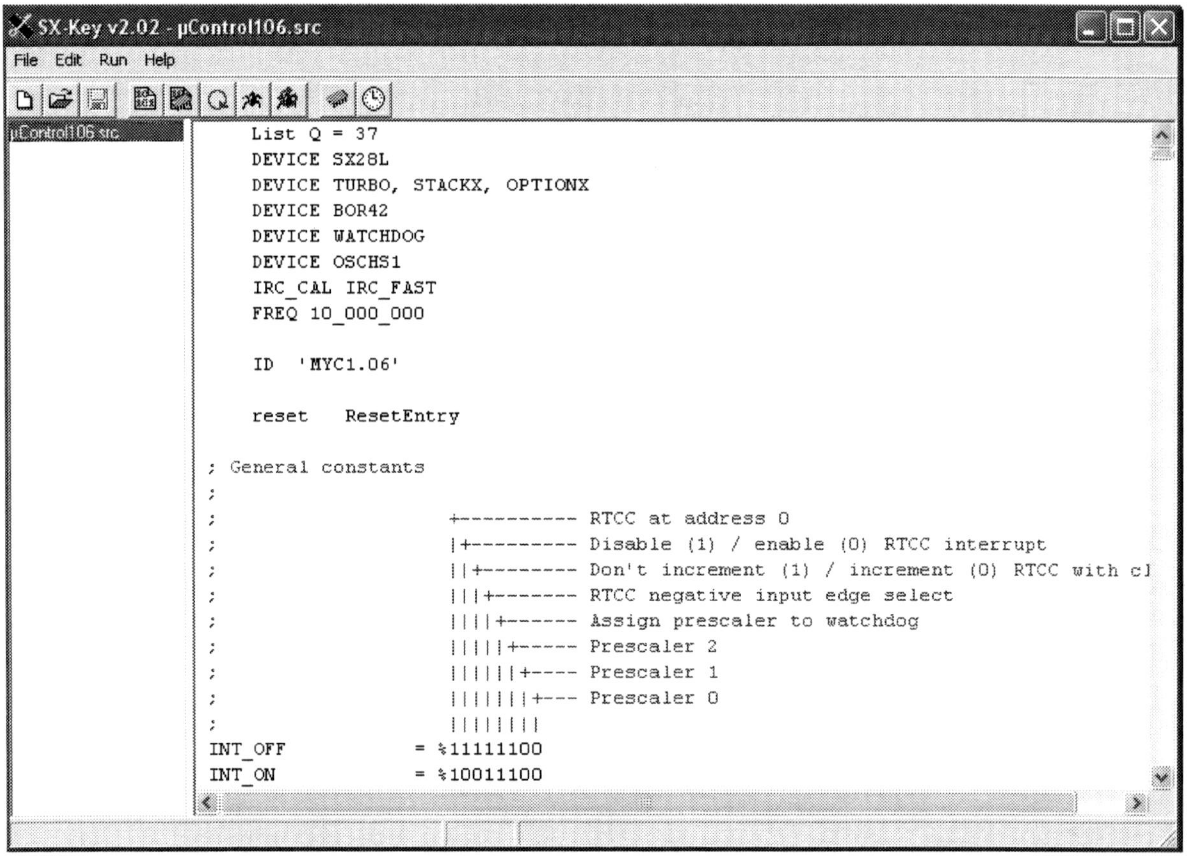

The SX editor (see Figure 6 – **The SX Editor**, above) consists of a window containing a menu at the top, several shortcut buttons in a tool bar, a list of files that are currently open to the left, and a large text area to the right. In the status bar at the bottom, there is the row/column indicator, telling you at which row and column the cursor is currently located. The editor window is where your SX source code will be entered and edited. Standard Windows editing shortcut keys listed in **Table 1 – Editor Shortcut Keys**, below, may be used in addition to the commands in the Edit menu and the tool bar buttons to manipulate the source code.

Table 1 - Editor Shortcut Keys

Function Name	Shortcut Keys	Function Description
Copy	Ctrl-C	Copies selected text to the clipboard.
Cut	Ctrl-X	Cuts selected text to the clipboard.
Paste	Ctrl-V	Pastes clipboard contents.
Page Up	PgUp	Moves editor window one page up.
Page Down	PgDn	Move editor window one page down.
Begin of Line	Home	Move the cursor to column 1 in the current line
End of Line	End	Move the cursor behind the last character in the line.
Begin of Text	Ctrl-Home	Moves the cursor to row 1, column 1 in the editor window.
End of Text	Ctrl-End	Moves the cursor behind the last character of the text in the editor.
Tab	Tab	Moves cursor to the next tab position. The tab position can be set in the configuration dialog.

4.3 The Menus

The SX editor menu bar contains four menus: *File, Edit, Run* and *Help*. These menus and their associated menu items are each described below. The most important functions can be also selected with one of the shortcut buttons in the tool bar that are also shown below. You will find details to some of the functions that can be selected via the menus later in this manual.

4.3.1 The File Menu

New

Creates a new, empty edit window. Use this item to start a new source code editing session. You may also click the shortcut button to create a new file. When you start the editor software, a blank session will be opened automatically, called "Blank 1".

When you select "New" while another editing session is already open, it will be moved to the "background" but it will still remain open. The open files list to the left displays the names of all open sessions.

Open...

Opens a browse window to locate and load source code files. As an alternative, click the shortcut button, or type Ctrl-O to open an existing file.

Again, if there is another session already open, it will be moved to the background.

The names of all currently open files are listed in the open files list to the left of the editor window. To switch between the sessions, left-click on the name of the file you want to see in the foreground.

Close — Closes the source code file currently displayed in the editor window. You may also right-click on the file name in the open files list, and then left-click on the prompt that is displayed to close a file.

When the file to be closed has been modified since the last save, a dialog box will open allowing you to select whether or not to save the file or abort the close operation; i.e. keep the file open in the editor.

Save — Saves the source code file currently displayed in the editor window. The shortcut button or Ctrl-S can also be used to save the file.

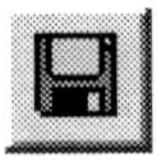

Save As… — Opens a Save As dialog box to save the source code currently displayed in the editor window with a designated name.

Reopen — Displays a list of the files that were most recently edited. You may then click on one of the list items to open any of these files directly.

Print… — Opens a print dialog box to print the source code currently displayed in the editor window.

Exit — Terminates the SX-Key/Blitz editor.

4.3.2 The Edit Menu

Undo — This menu selection remains inactive until you make a change to the text in the editor window. You can then revert the recent changes you have made to the text. Ctrl-Z also activates the Undo function.

Redo — This is the opposite of the Undo function. It allows you to restore any changes that were reverted by previous Undo actions. This selection remains inactive until you have used the Undo function at least once. Ctrl-Y also does a redo. After you have re-done an operation, you may undo it again.

Cut — Cuts the selected text from the editor window and stores it in the Windows clipboard. Ctrl-X is the equivalent keyboard entry.

To select text, use one of the standard Windows methods, like moving the mouse pointer across the text to be marked with the left mouse button pressed, or move the cursor with the cursor keys while the Shift key is held down.

In order to select complete lines in the text, move the mouse cursor to the left margin of the text area until it turns into an arrow, and then click the left mouse button. To mark two or more lines, mark the first line, and then drag the mouse up or down.

Copy

Copies the selected text from the editor window and stores it in the Windows clipboard. Ctrl-C is the equivalent keyboard entry.

Paste

Pastes the text from the Windows clipboard into the editor window starting at the current cursor location. Alternatively, type Ctrl-V to paste text.

Find

Opens the Find dialog box. Ctrl-F is the shortcut key for this function. Enter the text (or part of it) you are looking for. If necessary, you may select the options to search for whole words only, or to match upper- and lower-case characters. You can also specify the search direction, i.e. if the search shall be performed beginning at the current cursor position towards the beginning or end of the text.

Find Next

Finds the next occurrence of the specified text from the most recent Find operation. F3 also performs this function.

Find/Replace…

Opens the standard Windows replace dialog box. Ctrl-H is the shortcut key for this function. Again, you have the options to search for whole words only, or to match upper- and lower-case characters.

Go to Line Number

Opens a dialog box where you can enter a line number. Ctrl-G is the shortcut key for this function. Click "Ok" to close the dialog, and to position the cursor to column 1 in the specified line.

Clear Errors

When errors are encountered while assembling a source code file with the "new" default SASM assembler, the lines with errors are highlighted, and the errors found are displayed in the status area. Use this menu selection to clear all error information.

4.3.3 The Run Menu

Assemble

Assembles the code. You may also press Ctrl-A, or click the shortcut button to start the assembly. When the code in the editor window could be assembled without errors, the message "Assembly Successful" will show up in the status bar.

When you use the default "new" SASM assembler and if there are any errors encountered in the code, a message box will open, telling you that errors were found. Click "Ok" to close the box. At the bottom of the editor window, you will notice a new area that contains a list of all errors found during assembly. The first error message line is highlighted, and the offending line in the source code is also automatically highlighted.

When there are two or more error lines, double-click on a line in order to jump to the offending line in the source code.

Make the necessary corrections to the source code, and assemble the code again, until no more errors are reported.

The assembler may also generate warning messages that are shown in the same area, together with any errors. With warnings, the code will be assembled, but it is a good idea to make the necessary corrections to the source code in order to avoid warnings.

NOTE: Before assembly, the current file will be saved automatically. If you have entered code into a new blank editor window, use the Save function to save the window contents under a specific name before starting the assembler.

Program

Assembles the source code and programs the SX microcontroller (when the assembly was successful). Ctrl-P also starts programming.

Run

Assembles the source code, programs the SX and generates a clock signal. Ctrl-R also runs a program.

Debug

Assembles the source code, programs the SX, generates a clock signal and initiates the debug mode. (Not used on the SX-Blitz). Ctrl-D also starts the debugging mode.

Debug (reenter)

Assembles the source code, assumes that the SX device is already programmed with the recent code to be debugged (i.e. does not program the SX again), generates a clock signal and enters the debug mode. (Not used on the SX-Blitz). Ctrl-Alt-D also re-enters the debugger.

This option is handy when you have previously terminated a debug session that you want to continue later without having made changes to the source code in the meantime.

As long as you add, remove or change WATCH or BREAK directives in the source code, you may still use this function to reenter the debugging session without downloading the program to the SX.

Any other changes to the source code require a new download, i.e. you must use the Debug option instead, to start the debugger.

View List — Assembles the source code, and then opens another window that shows the contents of the list file generated by the assembler. Ctrl-L also displays the list file. The list file will be described in detail later in this manual (see **Chapter 7.10 – Files Created by SASM**).

Clock… — Opens the clock control dialog box to allow the modification of the clock activity and frequency. (Not used on the SX-Blitz). Ctrl-K also opens the clock dialog. With this function, the SX device's clock is supplied by the SX-Key, and you may test the functionality of an application at various clock rates.

Device… — Opens the device dialog box to allow modification of the SX microcontroller parameters. Ctrl-I also opens the device dialog box.

Configure… — Opens the configuration dialog box to allow modification of the SX-Key/Blitz programming interface. See **Chapter 4.4.5 – Configure Window** for configuration details. Ctrl-U also performs this operation.

4.3.4 The Help Menu

Contents — Displays information on how to use the WATCH and BREAK directives.

About — Displays the SX-Key/Blitz Development System information box.

4.4 The Windows

Many menu items open up a separate window for further configuration or monitoring. These windows are described below.

4.4.1 Print Window

The print window is accessed via the Print… item on the File menu. It is the standard Windows Print dialog box that you know from other applications. It allows you to select which printer shall be used, and depending on the printer type, various options can be selected.

4.4.2 Find Window

Figure 7 - The Find Window

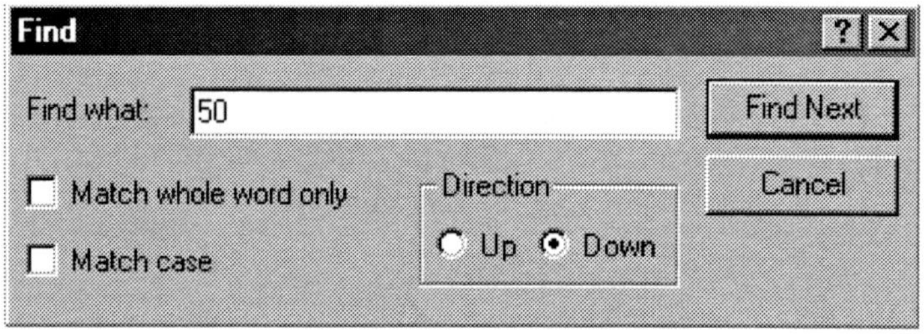

The Find window is accessed via the Find item on the Edit menu. Enter the text to be searched for in the "Find what" field. By default, the search direction is from the current cursor position to the bottom of the text. You may change this direction by clicking the "Up" radio button in the "Direction" group.

You may also specify if the search shall match whole words only and if upper/lower case characters shall be distinguished.

Click the "Find Next" button to start the search. When the pattern you have entered was found in the text, it will be highlighted.

Clicking "Find Next" again continues the search, and the next match will be selected in the text (if any). The Find window remains open, until you click the "Cancel" button.

After you have closed the Find window, you may still continue searching for the pattern most recently entered by selecting "Find Next" in the Edit menu, or simply hit the F3 key to continue the search.

4.4.3 Find/Replace Window

Figure 8 - The Find/Replace Window

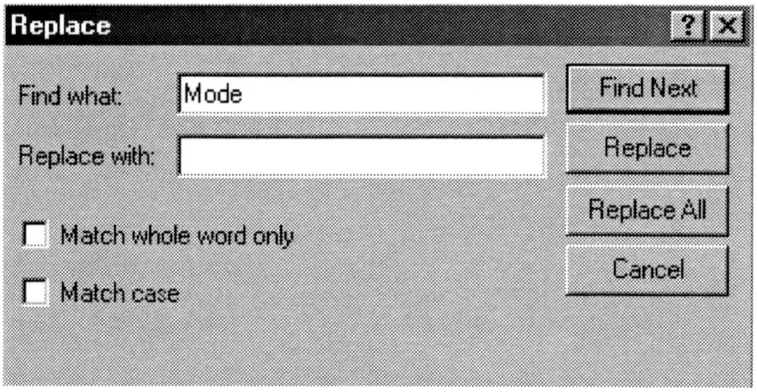

This window is similar to the Find window. Again, you can enter the text pattern to be searched for. In addition, you also can enter the replacement text.

Also, you may select if only whole words should be found and if the search shall be case-sensitive, or not.

Click the "Find Next" button to start the first search. When the pattern was found, it will be highlighted in the text.

Click the "Replace" button to replace the highlighted text with the replacement you have entered, or click "Find Next" to not alter the text, and to continue the search for the next matching pattern in the text.

When wish to replace all occurrences of the search pattern, click the "Replace All" button. You should use the replace all feature with extra caution because it replaces the search pattern in the whole text without further confirmation. You might consider activating the "whole words only" option to avoid unwanted replacements. Also note that "Replace All" always performs the search from the top of the text down to the bottom, where the find next always continues towards the bottom of the text.

4.4.4 Goto Line Number Window

Figure 9 - The Goto Line Number Window

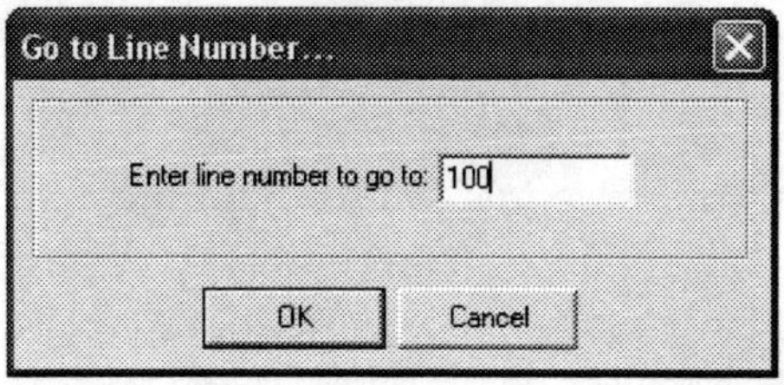

This window is accessed via the Goto Line Number item on the Edit menu. Enter the line number where the cursor shall be positioned and click Ok. If necessary, the text in the editor window will be scrolled so that the line you have addressed will be visible and the cursor is placed in column 1 of this line.

4.4.5 Configure Window

Figure 10 - The Configure Window

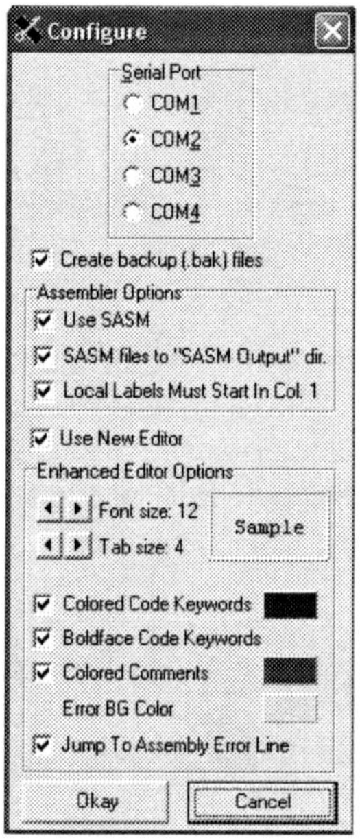

This window is accessed via the Configure item on the Run menu and allows you to setup various properties of the software.

We have already addressed the *Serial Port* section at the top of the window. Click one of the radio buttons to select the COM port where your SX-Key/Blitz is connected.

When the option *Create backup (.bak) files* is selected, the editor will save a copy of the previous version whenever a modified source code file is saved.

The group *Assembler Options* allows you to configure the SASM assembler.

When *Use SASM* is selected, the editor will call SASM to translate the source code in the editor window into SX machine code. SASM is an enhanced version of Ubicom's SASM assembler that has been adapted to the SX-Key Version 2 software. When you un-check this option, the original Parallax assembler will be invoked instead. Because there are some differences in language syntax between the two assemblers, it might be necessary to use the Parallax Assembler with older, legacy, source code (see **Chapter 7 – The SASM Assembler** and **Chapter 8 – The Parallax Assembler** for the differences between the assemblers).

Nevertheless, we strongly recommend that you use the SASM assembler for all new, or recently revised, source code. There are only a few modifications necessary to make legacy source code compatible with SASM (see **Chapter 9 – Upgrading Existing Code for SASM**).

When you choose to use the Parallax Assembler, by un-checking the "Use SASM" box, you will notice that a new group is shown at the top of the Options window, called *IRC Calibration*. Since the Parallax Assembler does not accept directives in the source code to set the value for IRC calibration, it is necessary to do this "outside" of the source code (see **Chapter 15.6.1.3 – Internal RC Mode** for details on IRC calibration).

When the option *SASM files to "SASM Output dir"* is selected, the files generated by SASM will be stored in the folder named "SASM Output" that is located in the folder where the SX-Key software has been installed. When the option is de-selected, the files will be stored in the folder where the source code files are located. See **Chapter 7.10 – Files Generated by SASM** for an explanation of the output files generated by SASM.

The option *Local Labels Must Start In Col. 1* controls how SASM searches the source code for local labels (see **Chapter 7.6 - Labels** for more details on local labels). When the option is selected, local labels must start in the first column of a source code line. Otherwise, local labels may be indented.

When the *Use New Editor* option is un-checked, the text editor will change its style into the editor format that was part of earlier versions of the SX-Key software. As this "old" editor has much less features, it is recommended to always use the "new" editor. You will notice that the remaining selections in the Configure window will become invisible when you select the "old" editor.

The *Enhanced Editor Options* group contains various selections that allow you to configure the "new" editor.

Use the upper left and right arrow buttons to change the *Font size* of the text displayed in the editor window between 6 and 32 points.

The left and right arrow buttons below let you define the *Tab size*, i.e. by how many columns text shall be indented on TAB characters in the text (2, 4, 6, or 8 columns).

When *Colored Code Keywords* is checked, the editor will perform "syntax highlighting", i.e. keywords in the source code text are displayed in color. Click on the colored button to the right of this option to open the Color dialog box. Here you can select the color that shall be used to highlight the keywords.

The *Boldface Code Keywords* gives you the option to let the editor display keywords in boldface. Boldfacing and color highlighting may also be combined.

When the *Colored Comments* option is checked, any comments in the source code text, i.e. text that starts with a semicolon, will be displayed in the color indicated to the right of this option. The color can be changed by clicking on the colored button.

The next option, *Error BG Color*, allows you to select the background color that shall be used to highlight any lines with errors after assembly. Again, click on the colored button to open the Color dialog box.

When the *Jump To Assembly Error Line* option is checked, the cursor will be positioned on the first line in the source code text after assembly, when errors were encountered. In addition, this line will be highlighted with the background color you have selected for the previous option.

After you have selected the required options, click "Okay" to accept them and to close the Configure window. Click "Cancel" instead, when you want to keep the options unchanged.

5 The SX-Key Debugger

The following is required to use the debug features:

- SX-Key Rev. E (or greater) – The SX-Blitz cannot be used for debugging.
- SX chip date code 9825 or later.
- No external clock source connected to the SX chip. This includes oscillator packs, crystals, resonators and RC circuits.
- The SX-Key connected to the 4-pin programming header of the SX system to be debugged.
- The SX system must be powered.

Source code to be debugged must include the RESET directive (see Chapter 7.3.21), must have WATCHDOG set to off, and must have 2 free words in the first page of code and 136 free words near the end of the last page of code (from 177 to 1FE, 377 to 3FE, 577 to 5FE, 777 to 7FE, 977 to 9FE, B77 to BFE, D77 to DFE, F77 to FFE), depending on the number of E^2Flash pages. If an oscillator frequency of other than 50 MHz (the default) is desired, the source code should contain a FREQ directive (see Chapter 7.3.9) stating the frequency. When the FREQ directive is missing, the assembler will generate a warning message, indicating that 50 MHz is used by default.

NOTE: On some machines, it is necessary to close background software (graphics, screen savers, etc.), for proper operation of the DEBUG windows.

In order to invoke the debugger, select "Debug" from the "Run" menu, press Ctrl-D, or click the debug shortcut button in the tool bar.

The source code that is currently displayed in the editor window will be assembled, and if no errors were found, the program is automatically transferred into the program memory of the SX device.

If the transfer was successful, and if an IRC Calibration setting of 4 MHz was chosen, a small window with IRC information is displayed. You may ignore this information for now, and click "Okay" to close the window (see **Chapter 15.6.1.3 – Internal RC Mode** for details on IRC calibration).

Next, the debugger will start, and the windows will be displayed as shown in **Figure 11 – The Debugger Windows**.

5.1 The Debugger Windows

5.1.1 The Registers Window

This window contains all the data and describes the current state of the SX chip. The leftmost column within the Registers window displays the hexadecimal contents of global registers $00 through $0F.

Registers $10 through $1F of all other banks are shown in the columns on the far right of the window. The bank offsets are labeled at the top of each column and the current bank is highlighted in white. These columns will expand or contract to fit the number of RAM banks available in the SX. In this example, eight banks are shown.

The blue outline, shown here on the IND register, indicates the location that the FSR (file select register) is currently pointing at.

The second column, just to the right of the first sixteen registers, displays a binary representation of some of the registers, namely IND, Status, RA, RB, RC and 08 through 0F.

At the top center of the Registers window are the contents of the M register (hexadecimal) and the W register (both hexadecimal and binary) and the Interrupt and Skip flags. The Interrupt and Skip flags turn blue when set and white when cleared. The interrupt flag is set when an interrupt has occurred and cleared after the interrupt has been serviced. The Skip flag is set when the compare condition evaluates to true, i.e. when the skip will be performed. It is cleared when the condition evaluates to false, or after the skip has been performed.

Figure 11 - The Debugger Windows

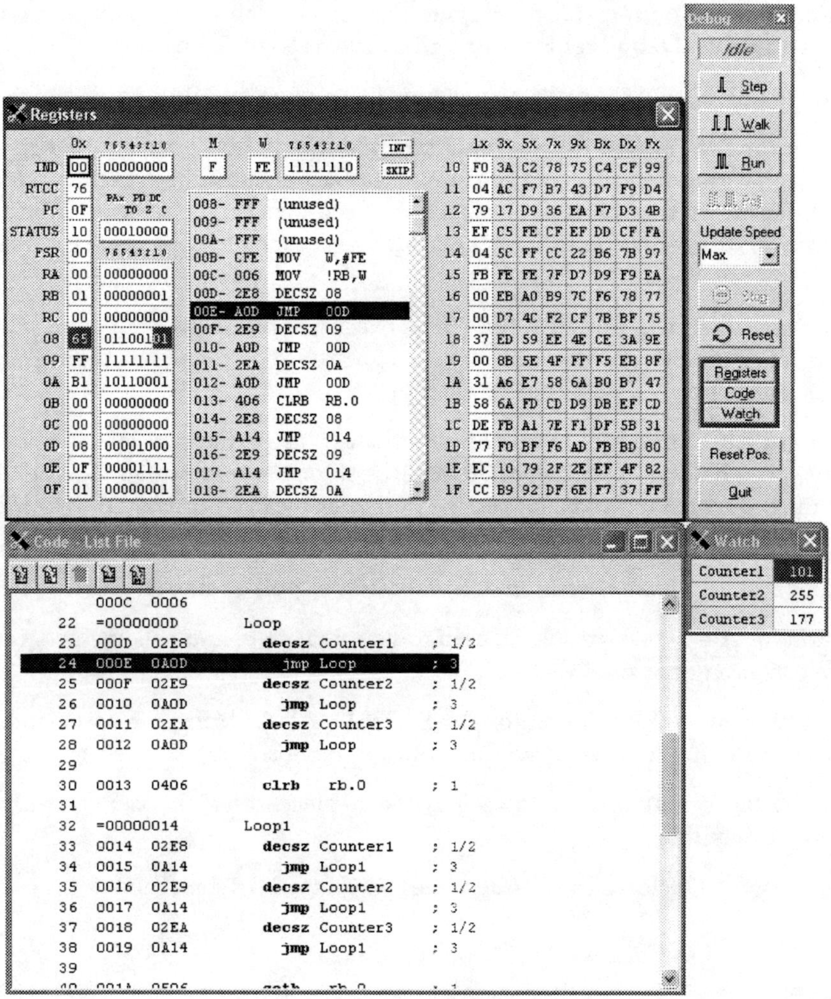

The *assembly code box* under the M and W register display in the center of the Registers window lists several contiguous instructions at once. The first three digits on each line is the hexadecimal address in program memory, followed by the opcode and finally the assembly mnemonic and operand(s). This window normally shows the active section of code, around which the program counter (PC) points, however, the scroll bar allows movement of the window's field of view to any section of code.

5.1.2 The Debug Window

The Debug window contains buttons for debugging functions. Each button has an associated shortcut key, as described in **Table 2 – Debugger Buttons and Shortcut Keys**, below.

- The *Step* button (or Alt-S) will execute one machine instruction and update all registers.
- The *Walk* button (or Alt-W) will execute one machine instruction after another in "slow motion", updating the display automatically and continuing until the Stop button is pressed, or a breakpoint is encountered. The delay time between instruction executions can be selected from the *Update Speed* drop-down list; with the range being from 1 (about one second) to Max (as fast as the computer can process it).
- The *Run* button (or Alt-R) will initiate a full-speed execution of the program, and will continue until a breakpoint is hit or the Stop or Reset buttons are pressed. The displayed registers will not update until the Poll button is pressed or execution is stopped.
- The *Poll* button (or Alt-L) operates in one of two modes. If a breakpoint exists, the Poll button runs the code at full speed halting execution at the break just long enough to update the display and then continues running. If a breakpoint is not set, the Poll button can be pressed only during run mode to get an instant update of the register displays.
- The *Stop* button (or Alt-P) halts execution of a walk, run or poll operation and updates the display.
- The *Reset* button (or Alt-T) returns the SX chip to its initial state and sets the program counter (PC) to the location containing the reset vector.
- The *Registers, Code* and *Watch* buttons (or Alt-E, Alt-D, Alt-C) bring the associated windows into view if they were hidden. (The Debug window always stays on top).
- The *Reset Pos.* button brings all windows into view, places them at their default positions, and resizes them to the defaults.
- The *Quit* button (or Alt-Q) closes the Debug windows and exits debug mode.

Table 2 - Debugger Buttons and Shortcut Keys

Button	Shortcut	Function
Step	Alt-S	Executes one machine instruction.
Walk	Alt-W	Executes multiple machine instructions in "slow motion".
Run	Alt-R	Executes instructions in full speed.
Poll	Alt-L	Updates display then continues execution. Can be used synchronously or asynchronously.
Stop	Alt-P	Halts execution of a walk or run operation.
Reset	Alt-T	Resets the SX chip.
Registers	Alt-E	Brings Registers window into view.
Code	Alt-D	Brings Code window into view.
Watch	Alt-C	Brings Watch window into view.
Reset Pos.	none	Resets all debugger windows to their defaults.
Quit	Alt-Q	Closes the Debug Windows and exits debug mode.

The Debug windows are highly active and interactive displays. Every time the display is updated (after a step, walk, poll or stop operation), each register that was modified since the previous update is highlighted in red. This provides a clear indication of what the last instruction accomplished. Similarly, each bit that was changed is marked in red within all registers shown in binary. Additionally, the assembly code box and Code window highlights the instruction pointed to by the program counter (PC) in blue, and a breakpoint in red.

5.1.3 The Watch Window

The Watch window displays the contents of selected registers in a user-defined format. The values in the Watch window can be modified using the same methods described in **Section 5.1.5 – Modifying registers during debugging**, below. In addition, the numerical values in the Watch window can be modified in any format (binary, hexadecimal or decimal) regardless of the displayed format. Simply precede the input value with a %, $, or nothing, respectively. String values can only be modified by entering new strings. See the Watch directive section in **Chapter 7.3.23 – The Watch Directive** for information of defining watches.

5.1.4 The Code/List File Window

This window displays the contents of the list file generated by the assembler (see **Chapter 7.10 – Files Created by SASM** for more information about the list file). While a program is executed in single steps, or in walk mode, the instruction that is currently executed is highlighted with a blue background.

If a breakpoint is defined, this line is highlighted with a red background.

The Code/List File window has a toolbar with several shortcut buttons. These buttons have the following meanings:

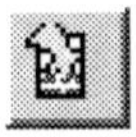

Jump to Code: Scrolls the window to display the first line that assembles into CPU instructions.

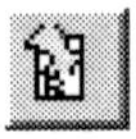

Jump to Reset Line: Scrolls the window to display the line of code that will be executed upon reset. This line will be highlighted blue.

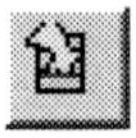

Jump to Breakpoint: Scrolls the window to display the line with the breakpoint. This line will be highlighted red. When no breakpoint is defined, this button is inactive.

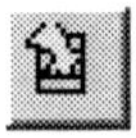

Jump to "Next Run" Line: Scrolls the window to display the next line of code that will be executed. The line will be highlighted blue.

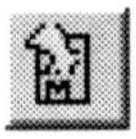

Jump to Main: Scrolls the window to display the label called "Main", if there is one.

5.1.5 Modifying registers during debugging

Any register, bits within registers, or flags can be modified using the mouse and keyboard (see **Table 3 – Register Editing Keys** for a summary of the editing keys). To modify a register (in hexadecimal), first click on it or use the tab and cursor keys to move the focus to that register. (The focus is indicated by a blinking, black highlight within the register). Next, type in the new hexadecimal value on the keyboard and press the enter, space, backspace or arrow keys to write the value to the register. The new value will appear in the selected register, highlighted in red to indicate a change.

To change a bit or flag in the binary registers, simply click the mouse on the appropriate bit. The bit will toggle to the opposite state and will be highlighted in red to indicate a change. Click on the INT or SKIP flags to toggle their state. The INT and SKIP flags, unlike registers, do not indicate a change with a red highlight. Instead, a blue color indicates the flag is set, while a white color indicates the flag is cleared.

If a register's contents are changed by accident, press the ESC (escape) key to restore its previous value.

Table 3 – Register Editing Keys

Key	Function
TAB	Move focus to new control block and ignore any changes to previous register.
Cursor Keys	Move focus to new register within control and write any changes to previous register.
Space	Same as cursor down.
Backspace	Same as cursor up.
Enter	Write changes to register.
ESC	Changes register value to previous value, if it has been changed by the user. This will not work if the enter, space, backspace or cursor keys have been pressed first.

5.1.6 Breakpoints and the Current Instruction

The assembly code box and Code/List File window display a breakpoint as a red highlighted line and the next instruction to be executed as a blue highlighted line.

The breakpoint can be set to a new line by clicking the mouse button once on the desired line in either the assembly code box, or in the Code/List File window. Clicking the mouse button again will remove the breakpoint. Only one breakpoint can be set at a time.

5.1.7 Setting the Program Counter

The next instruction to execute can be set to a new line by double-clicking the mouse button on the desired line in the assembly code box or the Code/List File window. Additionally, the program counter (PC) register's contents can be manually modified via the keyboard to set the next instruction to execute.

If a breakpoint and the program counter should both be on the same line, it will become multicolored. The first third of the line will be highlighted in red (to indicate the breakpoint) and the last two thirds of the line will be highlighted in blue (to indicate the next line to execute).

6 The Device Window

The Device window is accessed via the Device item on the Run menu, or by pressing Ctrl-I. You may also click the Device shortcut button in the editor's toolbar. This window allows you to specify all the device settings for the SX microcontroller you are using, program and verify or read the contents of the device and load or save object files for the SX.

Figure 12 - The Device Window

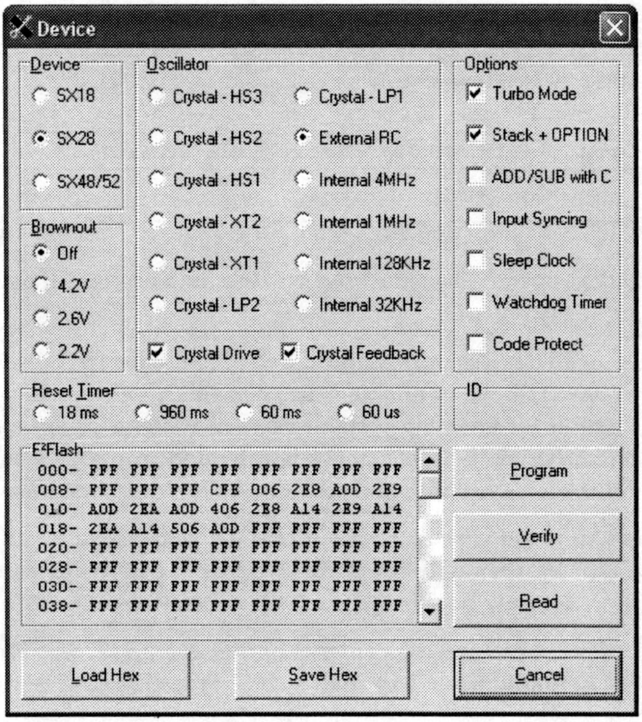

All data shown in this window reflect the settings specified in the DEVICE line(s) of the source code (if it had been assembled just before opening this window), the settings in the loaded object code or the settings read out of the device itself. You may modify these settings manually and program or reprogram the chip, however, those modifications will not be reflected in the source code.

The *Device* section (SX18, SX28 or SX48/52) should be set to the SX microcontroller that is currently used. It is important to make this selection first because depending on the device selected, some other options become active or inactive.

NOTE: To select an SX20 device, click on the SX18 selection. SX18 devices are no longer manufactured by Ubicom

The *Oscillator* section specifies the fuse settings for the various clock sources, and oscillator modes that are available in the SX devices, similar to the directives that can be given in the source code. Please note that any fuse settings defined in the source code will be overwritten by the options selected here when the SX controller is programmed from the Device window. See **Table 4 - SX Clock Options**, below, for a summary of the available clock options.

Table 4 - SX Clock Options

Setting	Description
HS1...3 XT1...2 LP1...2	Specifies the oscillator drive capacity for high speed, medium speed crystal/resonator, and low power crystal/resonator clocks.
External RC	Specifies special drive for external resistor-capacitor clock circuits.
Internal 32 KHz...4 MHz	Specifies internal clock at indicated frequency.

In the *Brownout* section, you can specify the threshold voltage for a brownout reset or you may also turn off brownout detection completely.

The *Reset Timer* section (SX48/52 devices only) should be set to the desired reset delay. The reset delay is the amount of time the SX48/52 waits after a reset condition before executing the first program instruction. This setting is useful for enabling a faster response after a sleep operation. It is critical to test this with your final circuit since the reset delay is intended to make sure the external oscillator (crystal, resonator, R/C circuit, etc) is running and stabilized before the first instruction executes.

The *Options* section allows you to set various fuse options. *Turbo* mode and enhanced *Stack + OPTION* can only be selected for SX20/28 devices because SX48/52 devices always have these options active, whereas the *Sleep Clock* option can only be selected for SX48/52 devices.

When you activate the *Code Protect* feature, the contents of the SX chip (except for the ID) cannot be read back once it is programmed. Actually, when you read a code-protected device, meaningless data will be read back instead.

The *ID* and *E²Flash* sections display the values contained in the ID and E²Flash memory (the program memory) respectively.

The *Program* button initiates programming the SX chip with the assembled source code or the object code loaded into the Device window.

Use the *Verify* and *Read* buttons to verify the code in the SX against that shown in the Device window or to simply read the SX's code into the Device window. These options are valuable should the code in an SX chip be questionable or unknown. Note that verifies will fail and reads will not reveal the true code or fuse settings if the SX chip was programmed with the code-protect fuse on. The ID field will always read properly, however.

The *Load Hex* and *Save Hex* buttons may be used to load or save assembled object files. If an object file is desired for a particular source program, simply load the source into the SX-Key editor, assemble it, open the Device window and click the Save Hex button. To program SX chips with an object file, use the Load Hex button on the Device window to load that file and then click the Program button.

Former versions of the SX-Key software had options in the Device window to set the IRC calibration, i.e. the calibration of the internal RC oscillator of the SX devices. This feature is now defined by a directive in the SASM assembler source code (see **Chapter 15.6.1.3 – Internal RC Mode** for details on the IRC calibration).

Click the *Cancel* button to close the device window.

7 The SASM Assembler

This part of the manual describes the SASM assembler (integrated in the SX-Key Version 2.0 software) which is an enhanced version of Ubicom's SASM.

The SX-Key software 2.0 and above supports both assemblers, the Ubicom SASM which is described in this chapter, and the Parallax Assembler which is described briefly in the next chapter.

Although you may select between both assemblers using the Configure dialog, it is highly suggested that you design all new code for SASM, and use the Parallax Assembler for "old" source code only, written under previous versions of the SX-Key software. You should even consider changing such code so that is assembles under SASM, or both because there are only a few minor modifications necessary for that purpose (see **Chapter 9 – Upgrading Existing Code for SASM**).

The main task of the assembler is to translate the contents of program source code files into code that can be programmed into the SX device's E^2Flash memory, where it is then executed at run-time.

The assembler also generates various output files that will be described in **Chapter 7.10 – Files created by SASM.**

7 The SASM Assembler

7.1 The Structure of an SX Assembly Program

A typical SX assembly language program contains comments, directives, symbols, labels, expressions and mnemonic instructions as shown in the sample below.

```
;-------------------------------------------
;|   XYZ Controller     Version 2.1        |
;|      (C) 1997 Company, Inc.             |
;|   Written by John Doe  12/01/97         |
;-------------------------------------------

; =====Device data and Equates=====
    DEVICE      SX28, OSCHS2, PROTECT
                ID'V2.1'
                RESET Main

pvdd            EQU   rc.1              ;vdd
data_out_a      EQU   %1100

; =====Variables=====
    org         $08                     ;point to start of ram

xbit_in         ds 1                    ;pc communication data
data_low        ds 1
data_high       ds 1
pulses          ds 1                    ;programming pulse count

; =====Begin code=====
    org         $000

; =====JUMP TABLE=====
    jmp         read                    ;$00 = read device
    jmp         program                 ;$01 = program device
    jmp         pin_mode                ;$07 = pin mode

; =====PC COMMUNICATION=====
get_data        mov   w,#19             ;ready
                clrb  dc                ;set receive mode
                jmp   send_data:bits    ;receive word into data

send_okay       mov   w,#$00
                mov   data_low,w
                mov   w,#4
                jmp   send_data:go

send_data       mov   w,#19             ;ready null+0+16outdata+1
                clc                     ;clear carry for stop bit
:go             setb  dc                ;set transmit mode
```

Comments

Directives

Symbols

Labels

Mnemonics

Operands

7.2 Comments

Comments are optional messages usually used to document the source code. They are ignored by the assembler and may be placed almost anywhere in the program. A comment must be preceded by a semicolon (;). The following demonstrates examples of comments.

```
; This program controls the GPX513v driver chip
;
mov counter, 120          ;initialize loop counter
```

Notice that a comment can be placed on the same line as an instruction (see the third line above). Since the assembler ignores everything that appears to the right of a semicolon, a comment may only appear on its own line or to the right of an instruction.

For debugging purposes, lines of code can be hidden from the assembler, or commented out, simply by inserting a semicolon before the first character of the line.

7.3 Assembler Directives

Assembler directives are special instructions to the assembler to help define symbols, set device options or indicate how the code should be assembled. Directives may appear within the source code, like assembly instructions, however, since they are instructions to the assembler and not the SX microcontroller, they are not actually assembled into the final machine language program. **Table 5 – SASM Directives**, below, describes the available SASM Assembler directives.

Table 5 - SASM Directives

Directive	Description	Syntax
= / SET	Assigns or reassigns a value to a symbol. This directive is used to create and manipulate assemble-time variables.	symbol = value
BREAK	Defines a run-time breakpoint.	BREAK
CASE / NOCASE	Specifies that the following instructions should be, or should not be, case sensitive.	{NO}CASE
DEVICE / FUSES / PROCESSOR	Sets SX device options. These directives usually precede all other directives and instructions.	DEVICE setting {,setting…}
DS / RES / ZERO	Increments the memory pointer ($) by value. Used to reserve RAM and E^2Flash during assembly.	symbol DS value
DW	Defines words in EEPROM.	DW data {,data…}
END	Marks the end of the source code. All text following the END will be ignored by the assembler.	END
EQU / GLOBAL	Assigns a value to a symbol. This directive is used to create assemble-time variables.	symbol EQU value
ERROR	Defines an assemble-time error or warning.	ERROR 'error text'
EXPAND / NOEXPAND	Specifies that the following macro instructions should be, or should not be, expanded in the list file. (See section **7.4.5 – The EXPAND and NOEXPAND Directives** for a detailed description.)	{NO}EXPAND
FREQ	Specifies the clock frequency, in Hz, to be generated by the SX-Key during debugging.	FREQ n
__FUSE / __FUSEX	Defines FUSE and FUSEX words as explicit expression values. Not recommended for use.	__FUSE expression __FUSEX expression
ID	Assigns a value to the 8-byte ID word in the SX. The text argument may be up to 8 characters and should be enclosed in apostrophes.	ID 'text'
IF {ELSE} ENDIF	Conditional assembly and alternate conditional assembly block.	IF condition {ELSE} ENDIF
IFDEF/IFNDEF {ELSE} ENDIF	Conditional assembly and alternate conditional assembly block based upon symbol definitions.	IF{N}DEF symbol {ELSE} ENDIF
INCLUDE	Includes a source code file, i.e. the INCLUDE directive is replaced by the contents of the file specified with the directive.	INCLUDE "<file path>"
IRC_CAL	Specifies the calibration value for the internal RC oscillator.	IRC_CAL IRC_SLOW | IRC_4MHZ | IRC_FAST
LIST	Controls the list format, and sets certain options	LIST {C=cols} {F=format} {L=NONE | NOPAGE | PAGE} {N=lines} {P=processor} {Q=message number} {R=radix} {X=ON | OFF}
LOCAL	Declares the labels named after the directive as private symbols that are only available inside a macro body. (See section **7.4.4 – The LOCAL directive** for a detailed description.)	LOCAL <label>[, <label>]…
LPAGE	Inserts a form feed at this point in the list file.	LPAGE
MACRO {EXITM} ENDM	Defines a macro. (See section **7.4 – Macros** for a detailed description.)	label MACRO {value} {EXITM} ENDM

Directive	Description	Syntax
ORG	Specifies the starting RAM or EEPROM location of the code that follows.	ORG value
RADIX	Specifies the radix for numeric constants	RADIX B | BIN | O | OCT | D | DEC | H | HEX
REPT ENDR	Repeat block of code a specified number of times.	REPT count ENDR
RESET	Specifies the starting location of the program in the SX's memory.	RESET label
SPAC	Inserts blank lines in the listing file	SPAC <number>
STITLE	Synonym for TITLE	STITLE "<string>"
TITLE	Defines a program listing title	TITLE "<string>"
WATCH	Defines a symbol to watch during debugging.	WATCH addr, count, format

7.3.1 The EQU and = Directives

The EQU (equate) directive defines symbols for constants. See the section entitled "Symbols" for further details. Instead of EQU, you may alternatively use the word GLOBAL; it has the same meaning.

The = (equal) directive defines symbols for constants or assemble-time variables. This directive is similar to EQU except that any symbols created with the = directive can be reassigned new values during assemble-time with additional = directives. See section 7.5 for further details. Instead of an equals sign, you may alternatively use the word SET; it has the same meaning.

7.3.2 The BREAK Directive

The BREAK directive causes a breakpoint to be set at the first line of executable code immediately following it. This is used to set and save a breakpoint in the source code in order to avoid the need to manually set a breakpoint in the Debug window. The syntax of the break directive is:

```
BREAK
breakpoint code
```

where *breakpoint code* is the desired line of source code to break on. The BREAK directive is ignored during any operation other than Debug. Only one breakpoint can be defined at a time.

7.3.3 The CASE and NOCASE Directives

The CASE and NOCASE directives specify how to handle the character case (upper or lower) of symbols in source code. The CASE directive will cause all the code below it, up to a NOCASE directive, to be case sensitive. The NOCASE directive will cause all code below it, up to a CASE directive, to be case insensitive. The default is case insensitive. The CASE and NOCASE directives can be used as often as desired and will only affect the code below them.

Using case sensitivity will allow symbols with the same name, but different character cases, to be treated as different symbols. For example:

```
CASE
temp        EQU $01
Temp        EQU $02
```

The above code would assemble properly and would have two distinct symbols, *temp* and *Temp*.

NOTE: All directives, instructions and reserved words must be specified in upper case when CASE is active. Using case sensitive mode can be very tricky, can easily lead to wasted time spent debugging, and is not recommended.

7.3.4 The DEVICE Directive

The DEVICE directive is perhaps the most important directive to appear in source code. This directive specifies the device type, oscillator type, brownout setting and more. The various symbols for specifying these options are listed in **Table 6 – SX20/28 DEVICE Settings** and Table 7 – **SX48/52 DEVICE Settings**.

Alternatively you may also use the words FUSES or PROCESSOR instead of DEVICE; they have the same meaning.

The device directive, if supplied, must be the first directive in the code, besides IFDEF or IFNDEF, and must appear before the first instruction. Multiple device lines can be used to accommodate many parameters as long as no conflicting parameters are given. The syntax of the device directive is:

```
DEVICE      setting {,setting...}
```

The following device lines tell the assembler that the SX chip to be programmed is an SX 20, will use a high speed oscillator, will initiate brown-out at 4.2 volts, runs in turbo mode, and is code protected.

```
DEVICE      SX20AC, OSCHS3
DEVICE      BOR42, TURBO, PROTECT
```

If a setting is not specified, the default is assumed. In this example, the device will also be set for 2-level stack, 6-bit option register, carry bit ignored, no input synching and no watchdog timer, since the opposing settings were not specified. See **Table 6 – SX20/28 DEVICE Settings** and Table 7 – **SX48/52 DEVICE Settings**, below, for the defaults.

Table 6 - SX20/28 DEVICE Settings

SX20, SX28 DEVICE Settings		
Setting	**Description**	**Default**
SX18/SX18AC/PINS18 SX20/SX20AC/PINS20 SX28/SX28AC/PINS28	Specifies the device type	SX18
BANKS1 BANKS2 BANKS4 BANKS8	1 page, 1 bank 2 pages, 1 bank 4 pages, 4 banks 4 pages, 8 banks	BANKS8
OSCHS3 OSCHS2 OSCHS1 OSCXT2 OSCXT1 OSCLP2 OSCLP1 OSCRC	High speed crystal/res., 1MHz...75MHz * High speed crystal/res., 1MHz...50MHz * High speed crystal/res., 1MHz...50MHz * Normal crystal/res., 1MHz...24MHz * Normal crystal/res., 32kHz...10MHz * Low power crystal/res., 32kHz...1MHz * Low power crystal/resonator, 32kHz * External RC circuit	OSCRC
OSC4MHZ OSC1MHZ OSC128KHZ OSC32KHZ	Specifies internal oscillator @ 4MHz Specifies internal oscillator @ 1 MHz Specifies internal oscillator @ 128 kHz Specifies internal oscillator @ 32 kHz	4 MHz
IFBD	Disables the internal feedback resistor, i.e. an external feedback resistor is required between the OSC1 and OSC2 pins	internal feedback resistor enabled
IRC_CAL	Specifies the calibration value for the internal RC oscillator, options are IRC_SLOW, IRC_4MHZ and IRC_FAST	IRC_SLOW
BOR42 BOR26 BOR22 BOROFF	Brownout to trigger at < 4.2 volts Brownout to trigger at < 2.6 volts Brownout to trigger at < 2.2 volts Disable Brownout reset	BOROFF
TURBO	Specifies turbo mode (1:1 execution)	Turbo off (1:4 execution)
OPTIONX or STACKX	Option register is extended to 8 bits, Stack is extended to 8 levels	Option 6 bits Stack 2 levels
CARRYX	ADD and SUB instructions use Carry flag as input**	Carry flag ignored
SYNC	Enable input syncing	disabled
WATCHDOG	Enable the watchdog timer	disabled
PROTECT	Enable code protection	disabled

* Any of these OSC settings may be used when an external clock source is connected to OSC1.

** Many instructions are adversely affected by the carry flag when CARRYX is specified. See Appendix B (Chapter 1) and Appendix C (Chapter 0) for more information.

Table 7 - SX48/52 DEVICE Settings

SX48, SX52 DEVICE Settings		
Setting	**Description**	**Default**
SX48/SX48BD/PINS48 SX52/SX52BD/PINS52	Specifies the device type	SX18
OSCHS3 OSCHS2 OSCHS1 OSCXT2 OSCXT1 OSCLP2 OSCLP1 OSCRC	High speed crystal/res., 1MHz…75MHz * High speed crystal/res., 1MHz…50MHz * High speed crystal/res., 1MHz…50MHz * Normal crystal/res., 1MHz…24MHz * Normal crystal/res., 32kHz…10MHz * Low power crystal/res., 32kHz…1MHz * Low power crystal/resonator, 32kHz * External RC circuit	OSCRC
OSC4MHZ OSC1MHZ OSC128KHZ OSC32KHZ	Specifies internal oscillator @ 4MHz Specifies internal oscillator @ 1 MHz Specifies internal oscillator @ 128 kHz Specifies internal oscillator @ 32 kHz	4 MHz
IFBD	Disables the internal feedback resistor, i.e. an external feedback resistor is required between the OSC1 and OSC2 pins	internal feedback resistor enabled
XTLBUFD	Disables the crystal drive (on OSC2 pin). Use this option to lower power consumption when using a crystal-oscillator-pack connected only to OSC1 pin.	enabled
IRC_CAL	Specifies the calibration value for the internal RC oscillator, options are IRC_SLOW, IRC_4MHZ and IRC_FAST	IRC_SLOW
BOR42 BOR26 BOR22 BOROFF	Brownout to trigger at < 4.2 volts Brownout to trigger at < 2.6 volts Brownout to trigger at < 2.2 volts Disable Brownout reset	BOROFF
CARRYX	ADD and SUB instructions use Carry flag as input*	Carry flag ignored
SYNC	Enable input syncing	disabled
WATCHDOG	Enable the watchdog timer	disabled
PROTECT	Enable code protection	disabled
SLEEPCLK	Enable clock generation during sleep mode	disabled
WDRT60 WDRT960 WDRT006 WDRT184	60 ms reset delay time 1 s reset delay time 0.25 ms reset delay time 18 ms reset delay time	18 ms

* Any of these OSC settings may be used when an external clock source is connected to OSC1.

**Many instructions are adversely affected by the carry flag when CARRYX is specified. See Appendix B (Chapter 1) and Appendix C (Chapter 0) for more information.

7.3.5 The DS Directive

The DS (define space) directive increments the location pointer during assembly. This may be used to cause the assembler to arrange sequential RAM assignments (arrays). For example:

```
        ORG             $08
Array                   DS  3
Other                   DS  2
```

defines 3 bytes, starting at location 8, for the *Array* symbol. *Array+1* is the second element of the array and *array+2* is the third element. The *Other* symbol's first and second elements are placed starting with location $0B. Note that no code is generated in the example above.

Instead of the DS, you may alternatively use the words RES or ZERO; they have the same meaning.

7.3.6 The DW Directive

The DW (define word) directive defines 12-bit words in EEPROM. This is used to store a data table in the SX EEPROM space. For example:

```
        DW              $FFF, $009, $1A0
```

stores the values $FFF, $009 and $1A0 into EEPROM starting at the current location. You may also use the DW directive to define a sequence of ASCII characters like in

```
        DW              "hello"
```

This creates a data table in the EEPROM containing the ASCII codes of the characters specified in the string, i.e. $068, $065, $06C, $06C, $06F. See **Chapter 10.5 – Creating Tables** for more information on using tables.

7.3.7 The END Directive

The END directive indicates the end of the source code in a file. Any text that follows the end directive is ignored by the assembler.

This feature is handy when you want to add any kind of comment text to the end of the source code file without the need to mark each line as a comment.

7.3.8 The ERROR Directive

The ERROR directive emits a user-defined message for this source code line. The syntax for the ERROR directive is:

ERROR [P1|2[W|C]]"<string>"

During assembly, SASM performs two passes through the source code. The optional first parameter can be used to control the type of message, and in which pass it shall be emitted.

P1 and P2 select the first and second pass; when the parameter is missing, pass 2 is the default. W defines a warning message, and C defines a comment. When W and C are omitted, the message will be an error. Assembly is stopped on error messages, but it continues on warnings and comments. Errors and warnings are displayed in the status area if the SX-Key software, where comments are only placed in the listing file.

Examples:

```
ERROR       "Message"    ; Pass 2 error
ERROR P1    "Message"    ; Pass 1 error
ERROR P1W   "Message"    ; Pass 1 warning
ERROR P1C   "Message"    ; Pass 1 comment
ERROR P2    "Message"    ; Pass 2 error (same as the default)
ERROR P2W   "Message"    ; Pass 2 warning
ERROR P2C   "Message"    ; Pass 2 comment
```

User-defined errors are particularly useful to provide usage checking for complex macros.

7.3.9 The FREQ Directive

The FREQ (frequency) directive is used to set the frequency (in Hz) of the SX-Key's internal programmable oscillator to be used during debugging. The syntax for the FREQ directive is:

```
FREQ        frequency
```

Note that *frequency* can be any number from 400000 to 110000000. Additionally, underscore characters can be used to help make the number more readable, as in 50_000_000, which is 50 MHz.

7.3.10 The __FUSE and __FUSEX Directives

These two directives allow defining explicit expression values for the two SX configuration registers, FUSE and FUSEX (note the two leading underscores in front of the directive names). It is **not recommended** to use these directives for setting the fuse bits directly. Instead, use the various other directives to configure the SX chip according to the needs of your application.

7.3.11 The ID Directive

The ID (identification) directive is used to write up to eight bytes of text into the ID word of the SX chip. This is used to record a version number or other unique identification for the code. This ID word can be read out of the SX chip at any time, regardless of the code protect setting. The line below will write *GPXv2.1* into the ID word:

```
        ID              'GPXv2.1'
```

7.3.12 The IF...ELSE...ENDIF Directive

The IF...ELSE directive is used to create conditional assembly blocks. A conditional assembly block is source code that is assembled only if the specified condition is true; otherwise, the code block is ignored by the assembler. Conditional assembly allows for easy code customization for multiple applications. For example, it might be necessary to produce a number of related products all based upon the same main source code but each having a small portion of unique code. The syntax for the IF...ELSE directive is:

```
        IF              condition
                        codeblock
        {ELSE
                        codeblock}
        ENDIF
```

Note that the ELSE block is optional and the ENDIF is required to end the conditional block. The comparison operators for the condition argument are listed in **Table 8 – Comparison Operators**, below.

Table 8 – Comparison Operators

Symbol	Operation
=	Equal
<>	Not equal
<	Less than
>	Greater than
<=	Less than or equal
>=	Greater than or equal

The following example demonstrates the use of the IF...ELSE directive.

```
Delay    EQU  10
Choice   EQU  1

IF       Delay >=9
         mov  $08, #5
         add  $09, #%011
ENDIF

IF       Choice = 0
         mov  $0A, #$1B
ELSE
         mov  $0A, #$1C
ENDIF
```

The condition for an IF...ELSE directive can contain expressions and multiple conditional statements. Two or more conditional statements may be specified by appending them together with the conditional operators NOT, AND, OR and XOR. For example:

```
IF choice = 1 AND delay > 9
```

would assemble the code block following it if *choice* equals 1 and *delay* is greater than 9 at assemble time. If the statement or expression evaluates to anything other than zero (0), the condition is true; otherwise, the condition is false.

7.3.13 The IF{N}DEF...ELSE...ENDIF Directives

The IFDEF...ELSE (if defined) and IFNDEF...ELSE (if not defined) directives are very similar to the IF...ELSE directive. The difference is they assemble or prevent assembly of code blocks based on whether a symbol is defined or not. For example:

```
DriverOn          EQU 1

IFDEF             DriverOn
{some code block here}
ENDIF
```

would assemble the code block in the IFDEF statement because the *DriverOn* symbol was defined. If *DriverOn* was not defined (i.e. line number 1, above, was commented out) the code block would be ignored.

Note that SASM considers labels to be defined when there is an assignment using EQU or "=" in the code before the IF{N}DEF directive, whereas the Parallax Assembler only accepts assignments using EQU.

With

```
DriverOn        =    1
```

the Parallax Assembler reports an "Expected a label" error.

7.3.14 The INCLUDE Directive

The INCLUDE directive allows the inclusion of one or more source code files in the main file that contains the include directive. Whenever the assembler processes an include directive, it replaces it with the contents of the file specified. The syntax of the include directive is:

```
INCLUDE        "<File Path>"
```

<File Path> must either specify a relative or the full file path, including the file name extension. For example, when the include file is located together with the main file in one folder, the directive could be

```
INCLUDE        "SX28Defs.src"
```

when the include file is located in a sub-folder of the folder where the main file is located, the directive could be

```
INCLUDE        "INCS\SX28Defs.src"
```

and if the include file is located elsewhere, the directive could be

```
INCLUDE        "D:\SXDev\INCS\ SX28Defs.src"
```

Please note that the path specification must be specified within quotes, and that the total length of the path specification may not exceed 63 characters.

It is possible to have more than one INCLUDE directive in a program and it is also possible that INCLUDE directives are used in include files, i.e. nesting of include files is allowed at a maximum level of 10.

When nesting include files, take care that files don't include themselves recursively.

Note: Any include files that are open in the editor are not automatically saved when you assemble the main file. Therefore perform a *Save* operation on any include files that you have changed before selecting the main file and do an *Assemble, Run* or *Debug* operation.

7.3.15 The IRC_CAL Directive

This directive specifies the calibration value for the internal RC oscillator.

The syntax for the IRC_CAL directive is

```
IRC_CAL        IRC_SLOW | IRC_4MHZ | IRC_FAST
```

When the options IRC_SLOW or IRC_FAST are specified, the IRCTRIM bits in the FUSEX device configuration register are programmed to the minimum or maximum frequency value. When the option IRC_4MHZ is specified, the SX-Key software performs a calibration procedure whenever a program is downloaded to the SX chip and adjusts the IRCTRIM bits so that the internally generated clock frequency comes close as possible to 4 MHz.

If you don't intend to use the internal RC oscillator, you should include an IRC_CAL IRC_SLOW or IRC_CAL IRC_FAST directive in your program code in order to de-activate the calibration process, which takes some extra time during downloading code to the SX device.

7.3.16 The LIST Directive

The LIST directive accepts various parameters to control the format of the list file and other assembler option.

The various syntax forms of the LIST directive are:

Table 9 - LIST Directive Options

Option	Meaning
LIST C = <columns>	Sets the number of columns in the list file (default: no column limit)
LIST F = <format>	Controls the output format of the HEX file – do not use this option because SASM creates the format required by the SX-Key software by default.
LIST L = <list>	Controls the list file output (default: NOPAGE): NONE = no list file PAGE = list file with page headers and form feeds, 55 lines/page by default (use LIST N to change the number of lines/page) NOPAGE = continuous list file with no page headers and form feeds
LIST N = <lines>	Sets the number of lines per page in the list file (default: 55)
LIST P = <processor>	Select the processor type. Use any of the following (default: SX18) SX18, SX18AC, PINS18, SX20, SX20AC, PINS20, SX28, SX28AC, PINS28, SX48, SX48BD, PINS48, SX52, SX52BD, PINS52. It is recommended to use a DEVICE directive instead, to select the processor type.
LIST Q = <message number>	Suppresses the output of the warning with the message number specified (default: output all warnings)
LIST R = <radix>	Use any of BIN, B, OCT, O, DEC, D, HEX, or H to specify the default radix for numerical values
LIST W = <0|1|2>	Controls which messages shall be generated: 0 = all messages (comments, warnings, errors) 1 = just warnings and errors 2 = just errors
LIST X = <on/off>	X = ON is a synonym for EXPAND (**see section 7.4.5 – The Expand and NoExpand Directives**) X = OFF is a synonym for NOEXPAND

7.3.17 The LPAGE Directive

The syntax for the LPAGE directive is

```
LPAGE
```

This inserts a form feed at this point in the list file. Note that the option LIST L = PAGE should be also active; otherwise, all form feed (including the ones caused by LPAGE directives) will be suppressed.

7.3.18 The ORG (Origin) Directive

The ORG (origin) directive tells the assembler the starting location to use for the following instructions. The syntax for the ORG directive is:

```
ORG          location
```

Note that the ORG directive does not dictate whether the location is in RAM or EEPROM. The assembler simply sets the location pointer as desired and the instructions or directives following the ORG will be processed in relation to this pointer. The ORG directive is used to place data and instructions at specific locations in RAM and E^2Flash.

7.3.19 The RADIX Directive

The RADIX directive sets the default for constants. The syntax is:

```
RADIX = B | BIN | O | OCT | D | DEC | H | HEX
```

The radix can be set to binary, octal, decimal, or hexadecimal. The default radix is decimal unless modified by a RADIX directive or by LIST R = <radix>.

Here is an example:

```
ORG     100     ; Sets the origin to 64 hex or 100 decimal (default radix is decimal)
RADIX = HEX
ORG     100     ; Sets the origin to 100 hex or 256 decimal (radix is hex now)
```

7.3.20 The REPT Directive

The REPT (repeat) directive is used to indicate that a block of code is to be repeated a specified number of times during assembly. The syntax for the REPT directive is:

```
REPT         count
codeblock
ENDR
```

Note that *count* must be greater than 0 and ENDR is required to end the repeat block. For example:

```
REPT         3
add          $0A, #$01
ENDR
```

would result in the source code being expanded to:

```
add        $0A, #$01
add        $0A, #$01
add        $0A, #$01
```

during the assembly of the code.

Within a repeat block, the percent sign (%) alone may be used to refer to the current iteration (1–n) of the block during assembly. For example:

```
REPT       3
add        $0A,#%
ENDR
```

would result in:

```
add        $0A, #1
add        $0A, #2
add        $0A, #3
```

during the assembly of the code. In other words, during assembly, the first time through the repeat block, the % symbol is equal to 1, the second time through it is equal to 2, etc.

7.3.21 The RESET Directive

The RESET directive specifies the starting address of the code to be executed when a reset condition occurs. The assembler places a 'Jump to Location' instruction at the last location in memory to facilitate this. The syntax of the RESET directive is:

```
RESET      location
```

The *location* argument must reside within the first page memory.

7.3.22 The SPAC Directive

The Syntax of the SPAC directive is

```
SPAC       <expression>
```

It inserts the number of blank lines given by <expression> into the list file.

7.3.23 The TITLE and STITLE Directives

The TITLE or STITLE directives set up the text to be used in the top line of the list file. The syntax is:

```
TITLE      "<string>"
STITLE     "<string>"
```

The text specified with <string> will be repeated on top of each page of the list file, provided the option LIST L=PAGE is active.

7.3.24 The WATCH Directive

The WATCH directive allows the definition of format for viewing and modifying variables at runtime during debug mode. The variable's bit address, number of bits or bytes to view, and display format may be specified. The syntax for the WATCH directive is:

```
WATCH      symbol{.bit}, count, format
```

The *symbol* argument can be a symbol name or register address and can optionally specify a bit address within the symbol. If no bit address is specified, bit 0 is assumed. The *count* argument indicates the number of bits (1-32) or bytes (1-16) to include in the displayed value. When using the FSTR or ZSTR format, the *count* is the number of bytes while in all other formats the *count* is the number of bits. Up to 32 WATCH directives can be specified. **Table 10 – WATCH Display Formats,** below, lists the available format settings for the WATCH directive.

Table 10 - WATCH Display Formats

Format	Operation
UDEC	Displays value in unsigned decimal format
SDEC	Displays value in signed decimal format
UHEX	Displays value in unsigned hexadecimal format
SHEX	Displays value in signed hexadecimal format
UBIN	Displays value in unsigned binary format
SBIN	Displays value in signed binary format
FSTR	Displays values in fixed-length string format
ZSTR	Displays values in zero-terminated format with maximum size

The WATCH directive may be specified anywhere in the source code, below a symbol's definition; however, it is suggested that it be specified near the top, below where symbols are defined. When code containing one or more WATCH directives is assembled and programmed using Debug mode, a Watch window appears, along with the other debugging windows, to display the results. The Watch window display is updated at the same time the Registers and Code windows are updated. Typically, WATCH directives are used in conjunction with the BREAK directive, however, asynchronous breaks and polls (with the Poll button) may be used to update the display as well.

The following code snippet is an example of multiple WATCH directives and their output:

```
        LCounter    EQU $08
        Hcounter    EQU $09
        Flags       EQU $0A
        String      EQU $0B              ; (3 chars, $0B - $0D)
        WATCH       LCounter, 16, UDEC
        WATCH       Flags.0, 1, UBIN
        WATCH       Flags.1, 1, UBIN
        WATCH       String, 3, FSTR

Start                                    ; Start of main routine
        MOV         LCounter, #$10
        MOV         HCounter, #$F0
        MOV         Flags, #%01
        MOV         String, #'H'
        MOV         String+1, #'I'
        MOV         String+2, #'!'
```

This code snippet would result in a Watch window similar to **Figure 13 – The Watch Window**, below:

Figure 13 - The Watch Window

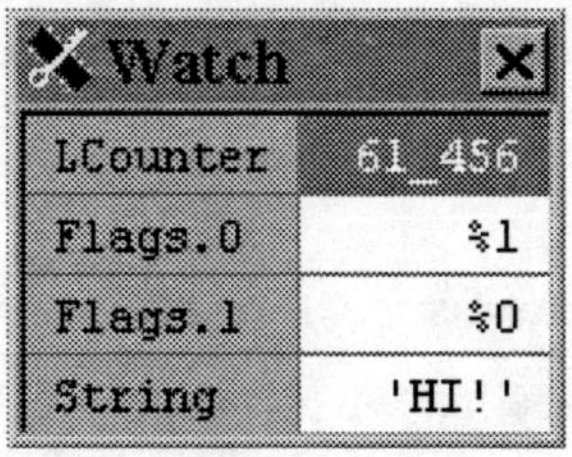

The first variable in the Watch window is created by the WATCH directive on line 5 of the source code. It tells the SX-Key to display a value starting at bit 0 of LCounter (since bit 0 is assumed if no bit address is specified) containing 16 bits and formatted as an unsigned decimal number. Note that although LCounter is only an 8-bit register, the WATCH directive can span multiple registers (from low-byte to high-byte) in order to construct up to a 32-bit value. In this case, LCounter ($08) is the lower 8 bits and HCounter ($09) is the upper 8 bits of the displayed value (61,456 or $F010).

The second and third variables in the Watch window are created by the WATCH directives on lines 6 and 7 of the source code. Both are single bit values, shown in unsigned binary format. The first of these corresponds to Flags' bit 0 (Flags.0) and the second corresponds to Flags' bit 1 (Flags.1) as specified by the *symbol* arguments.

The fourth variable in the Watch window is created by the last WATCH directive. It tells the SX-Key to display a fixed-length string (FSTR) of 3 bytes starting with the String symbol. In this case, 'HI!' is displayed.

If the ZSTR format is used, the Watch window will display all bytes up to a byte equal to zero, or up to the maximum length (specified by the *count* argument).

The values in the Watch window can be modified just like registers in the Registers window. See Modifying Registers During Debugging in Chapter 5.1.5 for more information.

7.4 Macros

Macros enhance the capabilities of the assembly language by allowing a user to collect useful sequences of instructions such that they may be inserted in a program easily. These sequences may include parameters that are specified at each invocation to modify the inserted instructions to suit a purpose.

Before a macro can be used, it must be defined. Each macro has a unique name, and may include named formal parameters, unnamed parameters, or no parameters at all.

A macro is defined with the MACRO, EXITM, and ENDM directives. The MACRO directive names the macro and describes its parameters. The ENDM directive marks the end of the definition. An EXITM directive may optionally appear in the macro body to mark a point at which later the use or insertion of the body will be terminated. The macro body consists of all lines extending from the MARCO directive to the next ENDM directive.

Macro definitions may not be nested. That is, it is not possible to write a macro which, when invoked, defines another macro.

7.4.1 The MACRO Directive

The MACRO directive takes one of three forms:

```
<label>        MACRO        <formal1>[, <formal2>, ...]
<label>        MACRO        <count>
<label>        MACRO
```

In all forms, the label names the macro. Macro names must be unique and follow the rules for any symbol name.

In the first form, the macro requires a specific number of parameters, which are given symbolic names. Every invocation must match the number of parameters used in the declaration.

In the second form, requires a specific number of parameters, none of which are named. Use zero for the count to declare a macro which must not take any parameters when invoked. Every invocation must match the specified number of parameters.

In the third form, the macro allows a variable number of parameters, none of which are named. Within the macro body, \0 will be replaced by the number of parameters actually supplied by the invocation.

7.4.2 The ENDM Directive

The ENDM directive takes the form:

```
ENDM
```

It simply marks the end of the macro declaration.

7.4.3 The EXITM Directive

The EXITM directive takes the form

```
EXITM
```

If assembled, it causes an invocation to stop interpolating lines of the macro body at this point. This is sometimes useful when building complex macros. In most cases, the EXITM directive should be placed within an IF, IFDEF, or IFNDEF structure.

7.4.4 The LOCAL Directive

The syntax for the LOCAL directive is

```
LOCAL          <label>[, <label>]...
```

It declares the labels named after the directive as private symbols. Private symbols are available only inside a macro body. These symbols are private to each invocation of the particular macro and cannot be referenced outside of the macro body.

The private symbol is used within a macro body just like any other label. Each time the macro is invoked, SASM will assign each private symbol a unique name of the form ??0001, ??0002, ??0003, and so forth. The unique name will appear in the listing file in place of all uses of the text of the private symbol.

All LOCAL directives must appear immediately after the MACRO directive and before the first actual line of the macro body.

7.4.5 The EXPAND and NOEXPAND Directives

The EXPAND and NOEXPAND directives specify how to handle macro calls for the purposes of list generation. If a list file is needed that has no macro mnemonics expanded, simply place the noexpand directive above the first macro call. The expand and noexpand directives can be used as often as desired and will only affect the code below them. For example, if source code referenced two macros, M1 and M2, and a list file was needed with only the M1 macro expanded, the expand/noexpand directives might be used as follows:

{macro definitions and other code appears above this point}

```
M1              {arguments here}

NOEXPAND
M2              {arguments here}
EXPAND

M1              {arguments here}
```

The above code will result in a list file with the first and last macro calls expanded and the second macro call unexpanded. Note that expand is the default so the expand directive was not used above the first macro call. Additionally, the list file will always show addresses and assembly within a macro regardless of the use of expand and noexpand directives.

7.4.6 Formal Parameters

Formal parameters may be declared by count or by name. If the MACRO directive has one or more names as arguments, those names are the formal parameters. If it has a single constant expression (well-defined in pass 1) that is the exact number of arguments required, the formal parameters are unnamed. If the MACRO directive is not followed by either a constant expression or names of arguments, then any number of arguments may be passed, and the formal parameters are unnamed.

If the formal parameters are named, then any occurrence of a formal parameter name in the macro body will be replaced by the exact text of the actual parameter (defined below) from the macro invocation.

Formal parameter names are case sensitive. That is, a formal parameter named "Foo" on the MACRO directive will be matched by the string "Foo" in the body, not by "foo", "FOO", or any other variations.

Whether or not the formal parameters are named, any occurrence of a backslash ("\") followed by a numeric constant in the current radix will be replaced by the exact text of the corresponding actual parameter from the macro invocation. The sequence "\0" will be replaced by the number of actual parameters available.

In order for the REPT directive to be useful to scan all arguments of a macro, the sequence "\%" will be replaced by the exact text of the actual parameter corresponding to the current iteration of the enclosing REPT directive.

Note that the value after the backslash must be either 0, non-zero and positive, or the percent character. All consecutive digits up to the first non-digit character will be used to form the parameter number.

In all cases, parameter substitution will occur at any point in the input where the reference to a formal parameter is discovered. Parameter names are recognized when delimited by white space, the beginning of a line, a comment or end of line, or one of the macro operators or quote mechanisms described later.

Note that formal parameter substitution does not occur inside of quoted strings or comments.

7.4.7 Macro Invocation

Once defined, a macro is used by invoking it with appropriate actual values to be used in place of the formal parameters. When invoked, the macro body is interpolated in place of the invocation, with each reference to a formal parameter replaced by the actual value of that parameter.

The invocation has the form:

<macroname> <parameter1> [, <parameter2> ...]

where macroname must match the name of a previously defined macro, and the number of parameters must agree with that definition.

7.4.8 Actual Values of Parameters

The actual value of a formal parameter is the exact text of the parameter after leading and trailing white space characters are removed. Parameters are separated by commas. The last parameter is terminated by a comment or the end of the line.

If a comma or white space must be passed as part of an actual parameter, then the parameter value may be enclosed in curly braces which will be removed before the value is substituted.

Grouping with curly braces does not prevent any formal parameter (of an enclosing macro) inside the text from being recognized and substituted. Note that ordinary quotes in an actual parameter are preserved, and also prevent formal parameter substitution. See Section **7.4.10 - Quoting** on quoting.

7.4.9 Token Pasting

The token pasting operator may be used to concatenate a formal parameter to other text to form a larger token. The token pasting operator effectively works as a zero-width space character which provides an opportunity for the formal parameter reference to be seen, and disappears from the source text for all further processing.

The notation C<token??token> will "paste" the two tokens together into a single token. Either token may be the name of a formal parameter or an index of a parameter in the C<\1> notation which will be substituted by its actual value, or any other text which will be preserved. The resulting text is taken as a single token and must be legal at the point where it appears or a suitable error will occur.

Token pasting is useful for including an actual parameter value as part of an instruction mnemonic or symbol name.

7.4.10 Quoting

On a macro invocation line, curly braces have the effect of collecting all the text they contain as a single actual parameter to the macro. The actual parameter consists of the text enclosed by the braces, which are discarded. Note that if the invocation line is part of the body of a macro definition, any formal parameters in that text will be substituted before the text is used as an actual parameter.

Parameter substitution will occur at any point where the reference to a formal parameter can be identified, except within string constants.

The notation "?token" will treat the actual value of the formal parameter named by "token" as if it were a quoted string. This may be useful to use a parameter both as part of a string and as part of an operand to an instruction. This is implemented by quoting the actual value with ASCII unit separator characters ($1f), unless it is already so quoted.

Also, the notation "?(...)" is available to evaluate an arbitrary well-defined expression and use its value as the text of a single actual parameter. The value is converted to text in the current default radix.

7.4.11 Macro Examples

This section shows some selected examples on how to use macros. Nevertheless, the macro features offered by SASM are so powerful that this section can only cover a subset of what is possible.

7.4.11.1 Simple Macros with no Parameters

```
CtrlLedOn       MACRO
                      clrb      rb.0
                ENDM

CtrlLEDOff      MACRO
                      setb      rb.0
                ENDM
```

These two macros simply replace CtrlLEDOn and CtrlLEDOff in the source code by clrb and setb instructions, i.e. the sequence

```
CtrlLEDOn
call            Delay
CtrlLEDOff
```

is assembled into

```
clrb            rb.0
call            Delay
setb            rb.0
```

The advantage of using macros here, is that it is only necessary to modify the macro definitions when another port bit shall be assigned to control the LED later.

7.4.12 Macros with Formal Parameters by Count

The following is a sample for a macro with one formal parameter:

```
; Sets the bank appropriately for all types of SX controllers
;
_bank macro 1
  bank \1
  IFDEF SX48_52
    IF \1 & %10000000          ; SX48BD and SX52BD bank instruction
      setb fsr.7               ; modifies FSR bits 4,5 and 6. FSR.7 needs to be set
                               ; by software.
    ELSE
      clrb fsr.7
    ENDIF
  ENDIF
endm
```

This macro is useful to replace the BANK instruction in programs that shall be running on SX48/52 devices as well as on "smaller" chips. The BANK instruction only affects FSR bits 4, 5 and 6 but on SX48/42 devices, it is also necessary to set or clear bit 7 in order to switch between the upper and lower banks. So instead of using the BANK instruction to switch between banks, use the _bank macro.

When this macro is used in a program to be run on an SX48/52, it is necessary that the symbol SX48_52 is defined prior to the first invocation of the _bank macro.

The next example is a replacement for the MODE instruction:

```
; Sets the mode register appropriately for all types of SX controllers
;
_mode macro 1
  IFDEF SX48_52
    mov w, #\1                 ; loads the M register correctly for the SX48BD and
                               ; SX52BD
    mov m, w
  ELSE
    mov m, #\1                 ; loads the M register correctly for the SX20AC
                               ; and SX28AC
  ENDIF
endm
```

The MODE instruction has a four bit operand only which is sufficient for SX20/28 devices as they only use four bits of the M register, however, the SX48/52 devices have the added ability of reading and writing some of the port registers, and therefore use five bits in the M register. The MOV M, w instruction modifies all bits of the M register, so this instruction must be used on the SX48/52 to make sure that the M register is written with the correct value. So , instead of using the MODE or MOV M, #<lit> instructions use _mode.

When this macro is used in a program to be run on an SX48/52, it is necessary that the symbol SX48_52 is defined prior to the first invocation of the _bank macro.

7.4.13 Macros with Formal Parameters by Name

This is an example for a macro with one named parameter:

```
delay MACRO cycles
  IF (cycles > 0)
    REPT (cycles/3)
      jmp $+1                     ; delay 3 cycles
    ENDR
    REPT (cycles//3)
      nop                         ; delay 1 cycle
    ENDR
  ENDIF
ENDM
```

When invoked with

```
delay 7
```

the word "cycles" is replaced by 7 and the macro expands into

```
IF (7 > 0)
  REPT (7/3)
    jmp $+1                       ; delay 3 cycles
    jmp $+1                       ; delay 3 cycles
  ENDR
  REPT (7//3)
    nop                           ; delay 1 cycle
  ENDR
ENDIF
```

The macro operates by generating as many JMP $+1 instructions as possible to use the bulk of the delay at a cost of one instruction word per three clock cycles then make up the balance with NOP instructions. For example, delay 6 would not generate NOP instructions at all but just two jmp $+1 instructions, where delay 8 would generate two jmp $+1 and two NOP instructions. In case of cycles = 0, no code is generated at all.

7.5 Symbols

Symbols are descriptive names for numeric values. Symbol names can consist of up to 32 alphanumeric and underscore (_) characters and must start with a letter or underscore. SASM expects symbol declarations to start in column 1 of the program line. Symbols for constants are usually defined near the start of assembly source code using the equal directive EQU. For example:

```
loop_count      EQU 10
index           EQU $08
```

defines the symbol *loop_count* to be equal to the number 10, and the symbol *index* to be equal to the hexadecimal number 08. During assembly, everywhere the symbol *loop_count* appears in the code, the number 10 will be used. Similarly, the hexadecimal number 08 will be used in place of the symbol *index* during assembly.

Symbols are a great way to define names for registers and constants that would otherwise appear in many places of a program as just non-descriptive numbers. Assembly code that makes ample use of symbols is easier to read and debug and requires fewer comments.

The = directive also assigns values to symbols, but unlike EQU, can reassign values to those symbols. This directive is useful in macros or repeat blocks to create assemble-time variables.

For example:

```
Count           = 0
ORG             $20
REPT            5
                DW  Count + 1 * 2
                Count = Count + 3
ENDR
```

stores the values 2, 8, 14, 20 and 26 in memory locations $20 through $24 at assemble-time.

7.6 Labels

Labels are descriptive names that are given to sections of code. Similar to symbol names, label names can consist of up to 32 alphanumeric and underscore (_) characters and must start with a letter or underscore. SASM expects labels to begin at column 1 of the program line, unless the *Local Labels Must Start In Col. 1* checkbox is unchecked in the Configure dialog. Labels are used to direct code execution to specific routines, and are defined simply by specifying the label name before the routine. For example:

```
Main            mov  index, #15
                jmp  main
```

defines the label *Main* to point at the first line of code. Later in the program (the second line in this example) to continue execution back at the first line, the jump command is used with the argument *Main*. This is usually read as, "jump to Main."

There are three types of labels: *global, local,* and *macro.* A global label is one that is unique for the entire length of the code. No two global labels can exist with the same name. A local label is one that is unique for only a portion of the code and must begin with a colon (:). A local label can have the same name as one or more other local labels in a program but they must be separated by at least one global or macro label. A macro label is the name of a macro block (see the MACRO directive in **Section 7.3.15 – The Macro Directive**) and is unique.

Depending on the option you have selected in the Configuration window, local labels must begin in text column 1, or may be indented.

No macro label can exist with the same name as another macro or global label. Actually, when a program contains a macro definition, and you use the macro name as a global label by mistake, the assembler would not report an error, but insert the macro code at the location of the "global label". The following code demonstrates global and local labels.

```
main      mov       loop_count, #15       ; initialize loop_count
:loop     mov       $09, #100             ; set some other register
          djnz      loop_count, :loop     ; decrement loop_count,
                                          ; jump to :loop if not zero
continue  move      loop_count, #50       ; set loop_count to 50
:loop     djnz      loop_count, :loop     ; decrement loop_count,
                                          ; jump to :loop if not zero
          jmp       main ;start over
```

The example above contains two global labels, *main* and *continue*, and two local labels, both named *:loop*. The area between the *main* and *continue* global labels is where a local label can exist. Since the djnz instruction in line 3 references the *:loop* label, and line 3 is between the global labels *main* and *continue*, it will only jump to the *:loop* label at line 2 and not the *:loop* label at line 6.

You may also jump to a local label from "outside". For example, the instruction

```
          jmp       continue:loop
```

elsewhere in the above program example would cause the program execution to be continued with the

```
          djnz      loop_count, :loop
```

instruction.

Local and global labels are also allowed within a macro. It is suggested that global labels not be used within a macro, however, as that would prevent the macro from being called more than once.

7.7 Expressions

Expressions may be used within the arguments of instructions and directives to calculate values at assemble time. The use of expressions helps build more maintainable, easier to understand code. For example, if a program uses values that are all related to the same base number, it makes sense to include an expression crafted from that relationship. If a symbol *N* is defined as being equal to the base number 2, then N*2+1 and N*3 can be used to derive values related to it; 5 and 6 in this case. At a later time, it might become necessary to adjust the base value to 3 and since expressions were used to derive the related values, only the symbol *N* needs to be modified.

All expressions are evaluated at assemble-time only; they are never reevaluated during run-time. This means symbols for unknowns, such as registers (which change at runtime), can not be included inside expressions.

All constants and symbols within expressions may be 32-bit numbers and the result of the expression is a 32-bit number. Since the SX is only an 8-bit processor, care must be taken to extract the appropriate portion of the result for any particular operation. Table 11 – Unary Operators **and**

Table 12 – Binary Operators **describe the available unary and binary operators for use within expressions.**

Table 11 - Unary Operators

<table>
<tr><th>Symbol</th><th>Unary Operation</th></tr>
<tr><td>||</td><td>Absolute value</td></tr>
<tr><td>-</td><td>Negative</td></tr>
<tr><td>~</td><td>Not</td></tr>
<tr><td>\</td><td>Macro assignment</td></tr>
</table>

Table 12 - Binary Operators

<table>
<tr><th>Symbol</th><th>Binary Operation</th></tr>
<tr><td>+</td><td>Addition</td></tr>
<tr><td>-</td><td>Subtraction</td></tr>
<tr><td>*</td><td>Multiplication</td></tr>
<tr><td>/</td><td>Division</td></tr>
<tr><td>//</td><td>Modulus</td></tr>
<tr><td>&</td><td>Logical AND</td></tr>
<tr><td>|</td><td>Logical OR</td></tr>
<tr><td>^</td><td>Logical XOR</td></tr>
<tr><td><<</td><td>Shift left</td></tr>
<tr><td>>></td><td>Shift right</td></tr>
<tr><td>><</td><td>Reverse bits</td></tr>
<tr><td>.</td><td>Bit address</td></tr>
<tr><td>()</td><td>Sub-expression</td></tr>
</table>

Expressions are evaluated strictly from left-to-right, except when parentheses are present. The following code demonstrates some simple expression usage.

```
loop_count      equ  5*3
table           ds   5+(2*3)
mov             loop_count+10/5, #%01101
```

The second expression, above, will evaluate to 11; the expression within parentheses is evaluated first. The third expression, loop_count+10/5, will evaluate to 5; 15 + 10 = 25 / 5 = 5.

7.8 Data Types

The assembler "understands" four data types: decimal, binary, hexadecimal and ASCII. **Table 13 – Data Types,** below, describes these data types and their syntax.

For compatibility reasons, the notations xxxxb and xxxxh are also accepted for the binary and hexadecimal data types, respectively. It is suggested that all new SX assembly code use the notation listed in **Table 13 – Data Types.**

Any numbers that evaluate to a result greater than 32-bits wide will cause an error at assemble time. The largest number allowed is

4_294_967_295 decimal,

$FFFF_FFFF hexadecimal, or

%1111_1111_1111_1111_1111_1111_1111_1111 binary.

Table 13 - Data Types

Data Type	Syntax	Example
Decimal	Xxxx	1250
Binary	%xxxx	%01101010
Hexadecimal	$xxxx	$1AC6
ASCII	'x'	'S'

7.9 The __SASM Pre-Defined Constant

SASM has an internal pre-defined constant named

__SASM

(note that there are *two* leading underscores in the name). This allows the preparation of source code that can contain SASM-specific code, and code that might be relevant for another SX assembler (like the Parallax assembler) by using an IFDEF…ELSE…ENDIF block. Here is an example:

```
ifdef __SASM
        DEVICE STACKX
        IRC_CAL IRC_SLOW
else
        DEVICE STACKX_OPTIONX
endif
```

When you assemble this code with SASM, the directives in the first (ifdef) block will be read by the assembler, causing the use of an 8-level stack, and the expanded option register, and the RC clock calibration set to slow.

When you use the Parallax Assembler instead, __SASM is not defined, thus the device directive in the lower (else) block will be read, the DEVICE STACKX_OPTIONX directive, which is the correct syntax for the Parallax Assembler to use an 8-level stack, and the expanded option register. This also suppresses the IRC_CAL directive which is not supported by the Parallax Assembler.

7.10 Files created by SASM

When SASM successfully assembles a source code file, it creates the following files, located in the same folder where the source code file resides:

- List file (.LST)
- Map File (.MAP)
- Object file (.OBJ)

In addition, the editor creates or overwrites a backup (.BAK) file when the respective option is set on in the *Configure* dialog. The backup file is a copy of the previously saved source code file.

All files are named with the associated source code file's name, but with the extensions mentioned above.

The *List File* contains the original source code plus additional information. Here a part of a list file is shown:

```
155 =00000000         ISR
156 0000 001C               bank      Serial
157
158 =00000001         :RS232_Transmit
159 0001 0470               clrb      TxDivide.3
160 0002 02B0               inc       TxDivide
161 0003 0543               stz
162 0004 0670               snb       TxDivide.3
163 0005 0231               test      TxCount
164 0006 0643               snz
```

In the leftmost column you will find the line numbers of the source code file. The next column either contains a value (for lines with labels, EQU, =, ORG, etc. directives), or the instruction address (for lines that evaluate to executable code). When a line contains an instruction, the executable code is shown in the next column to the right of the address.

In the remaining columns, the original source code is shown.

At the end of the list file, there is a *Cross Reference* listing with all symbols used in the program, structured like in the following example:

```
__SX_FREQ          DATA   00989680   0008
__SX_IRC_CAL       DATA   00000002   0007
__SX_RESET         RESB   00000AA3   0012
_CheckEmergency    ADDR   0000033C   0787
ByteCnt            VAR    00000097   0124
fsr                RESV   00000004   0379
```

The leftmost column contains the symbol names, followed by the type in the next column (ADDR = label address, DATA = internal values, RESB = reset branch, RESV = reserved variable, VAR = program-defined variable or constant).

The next column shows the values of the symbols, i.e. an address, the constant value, etc., and the rightmost column lists the source code line number where the symbol is defined.

The *Map File* is not required by the SX-Key software.

The *Object File* contains an image of the generated code as it must be transferred into the SX device's program memory during downloads.

7.11 SASM Warning and Error Messages

SASM reports two types of messages during the assembly process: *warnings* and *errors*. Warnings are informative message about potential problems with the source code, but they do not halt the assembly or the download process. Errors are critical messages indicating syntactic problems with the source code. Errors prevent assembly from completing successfully and, if invoked, the download process is prevented as well.

While warnings can sometimes provide useful information, many times they can become a nuisance. Therefore, SASM allows warnings to be suppressed with the LIST Q directive. The format is as follows:

```
LIST Q = {warning number}
```

where *warning number* is the actual number displayed together with the warning message when it is not suppressed. For example, you might see a warning similar to the following:

```
...Line 15, Warning 37, Pass2: Literal truncated to 8 bits
```

If this warning tells you something you already know, and it is just a nuisance to you, use the warning number (37 in this example) in a LIST Q directive. For example, near the top of the code insert

```
LIST Q = 37
```

To suppress multiple warnings, such as #37 and #64, you can use the LIST Q directive in the format shown below:

```
LIST Q = 37, Q = 64
```

If you desire to suppress a warning only in a specific area of the code, you can surround the code like this:

```
LIST Q = 37
mov w, #-200
LIST Q = -37
```

The minus sign in front of the warning number will toggle it back to an active warning again.

The table below summarizes all error and warning messages of SASM:

Table 14 - SASM Error and Warning Messages

SASM Error and Warning Messages			
#	Message	Meaning	Type
1	Bad instruction statement	Misspelled instruction or incomplete instruction line	E
2	Redefinition of symbol <name>	The symbol is already defined with an EQU before	E
3	Symbol <name> is not defined	The symbol used in a statement is not defined before	E
4	Symbol is a reserved word	The name you tried to use for a symbol is a reserved word	E
5	Missing operand(s)	An operand is missing in an expression	E
6	Too many operands	Too many operands for this expression	E
7	Missing file register	Specification of a file register is expected	E
8	Missing literal	A literal was expected	E
9	Missing Label	A label was expected	E
10	Missing right parenthesis	A right parenthesis is missing in an expression	E
11	Missing expression	An expression was expected	E
12	Redefinition of MACRO label <name>	A macro with this name is already defined	E
13	Bad expression	An expression is incomplete or incorrect	E
14	Bad argument <text>	<Text> is not allowed as argument in this expression	E
15	Bad MACRO expression	A macro expression is incomplete or incorrect	E
16	Macro arguments do not match	The arguments passed to a macro don't match the arguments defined	E
17	Unmatched MACRO	A macro definition is missing an ENDM	E
18	Bad IF-ELSE-ENDIF statement	Illegal structure of an IF-ELSE-ENDIF	E
19	Unmatched ELSE	An ELSE without a previous IF was found	E
20	Unmatched ENDIF	An ENDIF without a previous IF was found	E
21	File nesting error - too deep	Check for recursive INCLUDES	E
22	If.else.endif nesting error - too deep	Nesting of IF-ELSE-ENDIF blocks too deep	E
23	Invalid digit in numeric constant	A digit in a numeric constant is not allowed with this radix	E
24	Value is out of range	Value too large or too small	E
25	Bad radix value	Only radix 2, 8, 10, or 16 allowed	E
26	Unknown microcontroller type	Invalid microcontroller type specified in LIST directive	E
27	Unknown output format	Bad command line parameter	E
28	Unknown listing parameter	Bad command line parameter	E
29	Bad string syntax	A string constant was specified with non-matching quotes	E
30	Overwriting same program counter location	Assembled code expands into an area that has been reserved for other code by an ORG directive	E
31	Expected an '=' sign	An equals sign is missing	E

SASM Error and Warning Messages			
#	Message	Meaning	Type
32	Unexpected EOF	The source code file ends unexpectedly.	E
33	Assume value is in HEXADECIMAL	No radix specified, hex assumed by default	W
34	Token length exceeds limit	Internal error	E
35	Illegal character - Ignored	An illegal character was found and ignored	W
36	File register truncated to 5 bits	Obsolete message	W
37	Literal truncated to 8 bits	A literal too large for the target was truncated, e.g. mov fr, 256	W
38	Missing RAM Bank bits	Obsolete message	E
39	No destination bit	Bit move instruction w/o target bit specified	E
40	Destination bit can only be 0 or 1	Obsolete message	E
41	Bit number out of range	A bit number > 7 was specified	E
42	Destination address not in selected page	Destination address for jump or call is outside of currently selected code page	E
43	Address exceeds memory limit	Address specified targets outside of the available memory	E
44	Address is not within lower half of memory page	Address of a subroutine call is outside the first half of a program memory page	E
45	Label must begin at column 1	An indented label was found	E
46	Ignoring unknown directive	Unknown directive is ignored during assembly	W
47	REPT count exceed limit	Only counts up to 254 allowed	E
48	File register not in current bank	An accessed file register is not within the currently active RAM bank	W
49	MODE register value truncated to 4-bits	Only the lower 4-bits of value are stored in MODE	W
50	Expected a fr.bit operand	Bad parameter for a setb/clrb instruction	E
51	Obsolete keyword: <text> for this device	For example, DEVICE TURBO specified together with DEVICE SX52	W
52	Reset address not in page 0	Address specified with RESET is not in the first page of program memory	E
53	Applied non bitfield operator to a bitfield value	Illegal bitfield operator	W
54	Overriding earlier target device declaration	For example, a DEVICE SX28 follows a DEVICE SX20 directive	W
55	ERROR <text>	Error message generated from the ERROR directive	E
56	Source line is too long	The length of the source line exceeds 256 characters	E
57	Local symbol <text> expands to more than 130 characters	Local symbols are internally stored as "Global:Local", where "Global" is the name of the previous global symbol, and the total length may not exceed 130 characters.	E
58	Division by zero	Zero-division is in an expression	E
59	Literal truncated to 12 bits	Only the lower 12-bits of value are used in instruction	W
60	Couldn't open file: <name>	SASM was unable to open a source file	E
61	Couldn't open include file: <name>	SASM was unable to open an include file	E
62	Include path and file exceeds 64 characters	The full path and filename of an include file was longer than 64 characters	E
63	WATCH is missing parameters	A WATCH directive was missing some parameters	E
64	IRC_CAL has invalid or missing parameters	The IRC_CAL directive was incorrectly written	E
65	No IRC_CAL directive. Default IRC_SLOW being used	There was no IRC_CAL directive. The default of IRC_SLOW is being used	W
66	No FREQ directive. Default 50 MHz being used	There was no FREQ directive. The default of 50 MHz is being used	W

SASM Error and Warning Messages			
#	Message	Meaning	Type
67	Total number of INCLUDE files exceeded 31	No more than 31 include files allowed	E
68	Tab expanded list file line too long – truncating	SASM internally converts any tabs into spaces, and it does this based on the tab setting passed to it. With a large number of tabs and large tab setting, it is possible to create an expanded version of a source line that is longer than the maximum length of 256 characters	E
69	No OSCxxx directive - using default OSCRC	No OSCxxx (e.g. OSCLP!, OSCHS, OSC4MHZ, etc) device directive was provided. The default of OSCRC is being used	W
70	USER WARNING: <Message>	Warning message generated from the ERROR directive	W

E = Error, W = Warning

7.12 Reserved Words and Symbols

Table 15 – SASM Reserved Words, below, contains all symbols that are internally defined in SASM, i.e. you may not use any of these words for labels or symbols in your programs. If you try to do that, the assembler will generate an error message.

Table 15 - SASM Reserved Words

__FUSE	CSB	INC	OPTIONX *	RESET	SX18AC
__FUSEX	CSBE	INCLUDE	OR	RET	SX20
ADD	CSE	INCSZ	ORG	RETI	SX20AC
ADDB	CSNE	IND	OSC1MHZ	RETIW	SX28
AND	DATA	INDF	OSC32KHZ	RETW	SX28AC
BANK	DC	IRC_4MHZ	OSC4MHZ	RL	SX48
BANKS1*	DEC	IRC_CAL	OSCHS1	RR	SX48BD
BANKS2 *	DECSZ	IRC_FAST	OSCHS2	RTCC	SX52
BANKS4 *	DEVICE	IRC_SLOW	OSCHS3	SB	SX52BD
BANKS8 *	DJNZ	IREAD	OSCLP1	SBIN	SYNC
BOR22	DS	JB	OSCLP2	SC	SZ
BOR26	DW	JC	OSCRC	SDEC	TEST
BOR47	ELSE	JMP	OSCXT1	SET	TITLE
BOROFF	END	JNB	OSCXT2	SETB	TMR0
BREAK	ENDIF	JNC	PAGE	SHEX	TO
C	ENDM	JNZ	PC	SKIP	TURBO *
CALL	ENDR	LIST	PCL	SLEEP	UBIN
CARRYX	EQU	LOCAL	PINS18	SLEEPCLK **	UDEC
CASE	ERROR	LPAGE	PINS20	SNB	UHEX
CJA	EXITM	M	PINS28	SNC	W
CJAE	EXPAND	MACRO	PINS48	SNZ	WATCH
CJB	FREQ	MODE	PINS52	SPAC	WDRT006 **
CJBE	FSR	MOV	PROCESSOR	STACKX *	WDRT184 **
CJE	FUSES	MOVB	PROTECT	STATUS	WDRT60 **
CJNE	GLOBALID	MOVSZ	RA	STC	WDRT960 **
CLC	ID	NOCASE	RB	STITLE	WDT
CLR	IF	NOEXPAND	RC	STZ	XOR
CLRB	IFBD	NOP	RD	SUB	XTLBUFD **
CLZ	IFDEF	NOT	RE	SUBB	Z
CSA	IFNDEF	OCS128KHZ	REPT	SWAP	ZERO
CSAE	IJNZ	OPTION	RES	SX18	ZSTR

* SX20/28 only, ** SX48/52 only

8 The Parallax Assembler

This chapter describes the Parallax assembler. We have added it for completeness, although we strongly recommend using the SASM assembler for new projects. You may use the Parallax assembler to re-build projects that have been developed under a former version of the SX-Key software. You should even consider changing such code so that is assembles under SASM, or both, because there are only a few minor modifications necessary for that purpose (see **Chapter 9 – Upgrading Existing Code for SASM**).

8.1 The Structure of an SX Assembly Program

The general structure of an assembly program for the Parallax assembler is identical to the one described for SASM in the previous section. Therefore, please refer to **Chapter 7.1 – The Structure of an SX Assembly Program** for details.

8.2 Assembler Directives

The Parallax assembler supports most of the SASM directives as SASM with the exception of GLOBAL, __FUSE, __FUSEX, FUSES, IRC_CAL, LIST, LOCAL, LPAGE, PROCESSOR, RADIX, RES, SET, SPAC, STITLE, SUBTITLE, TITLE and ZERO, and different options for the DEVICE directive.

Also, the MACRO and ERROR directives are a subset of those in SASM, i.e. some of the options in macro definitions are not supported by the Parallax Assembler.

8.2.1 The Device Directive

Table 16 – Parallax Assembler DEVICE Options, below, lists the available DEVICE directive options.

Table 16 - Parallax Assembler DEVICE Options

Setting	Description	Default
SX18/SX18L SX28/SX28L SX48 SX52	Specifies the device type	SX18
OSCHS3/OSCXTMAX OSCHS2/OSCXT5 OSCHS1/OSCXT4 OSCXT2/OSCXT3 OSCXT1 OSCLP2 OSCLP1/OSCXTMIN OSCRC	High speed crystal/res., 1MHz...75MHz * High speed crystal/res., 1MHz...50MHz * High speed crystal/res., 1MHz...50MHz * Normal crystal/res., 1MHz...24MHz * Normal crystal/res., 32kHz...10MHz * Low power crystal/res., 32kHz...1MHz * Low power crystal/resonator, 32kHz * External RC circuit	OSCHS2
OSC4MHZ OSC1MHZ OSC128KHZ OSC32KHZ	Specifies internal oscillator @ 4MHz Specifies internal oscillator @ 1 MHz Specifies internal oscillator @ 128 kHz Specifies internal oscillator @ 32 kHz	4 MHz
IFBD	Disables the internal feedback resistor, i.e. an external feedback resistor is required between the OSC1 and OSC2 pins	internal feedback resistor enabled
XTLBUFD / DRIVEOFF	Disables the crystal drive (on OSC2 pin). Use this option to lower ower consumption when using a crystal-oscillator-pack connected only › OSC1 pin.	enabled
DRT18MS DRT60MS DRT960MS DRT60US	Device reset timer waits 18 ms Device reset timer waits 60 ms Device reset timer waits 960 ms Device reset timer waits 60 us	DRT18MS
BOR42 BOR26 BOR22	Brownout to trigger at < 4.2 volts Brownout to trigger at < 2.6 volts Brownout to trigger at < 2.2 volts	no brownout
TURBO	Specifies turbo mode (1:1 execution)	1:4 execution
STACKX_OPTIONX	Stack is extended to 8 levels and Option register is extended to 8 bits	2 levels/6 bits
CARRYX	ADD and SUB instructions use Carry flag as input*	Carry flag ignored
SYNC	Input Syncing enabled	Input Syncing disabled
WATCHDOG	Watchdog Timer enabled	Watchdog disabled
PROTECT	Code Protect enabled	Code Protect disabled
SLEEPCLOCK	Clock is enabled during sleep	No clock during sleep

* Many instructions are adversely affected by the carry flag when CARRYX is specified. See Appendix B (chapter 1) and Appendix C (chapter 0) for more information.

Shaded areas indicate SX48/52-only directives.

8.3 Symbols

Symbols are handled by the Parallax Assembler similar to SASM. Therefore, refer to **Chapter 7.5 - Symbols** for more details.

8.4 Labels

Global, local, and macro Labels are also available in the Parallax Assembler. For more details about Labels refer to **Chapter 7.6 – Labels**.

Unlike SASM, global or local labels in source code for the Parallax Assembler may be indented, i.e. they must not necessarily begin in column 1 of a text line.

8.5 Expressions

Expressions are handled by the Parallax Assembler similar to SASM. Therefore, refer to **Chapter 7.7 – Expressions** for more details.

8.6 Error Messages

Table 17 – Parallax Assembler Error Messages, below, summarizes the error messages that might be generated by the Parallax Assembler in alphabetic order together with brief explanations in most cases.

Table 17 - Parallax Assembler Error Messages

Message	Explanation
"=" must be preceded by a variable	No valid symbol exists to the left of the "=". Check for mistyped symbol. Watch out for different case when the CASE directive is used. Make sure symbol is not a reserved word.
"\" only allowed in MACRO definition	The macro argument symbol, "\", is a meaningless character outside of macros.
CALL must be to first half of page	The destination address of the CALL instruction points to the second half of a page. See section 10.6.2 for more information.
Constant exceeds 32 bits	The SX-Key assembler can not handle constants whose value is larger than 32 bits or 64 digits.
Constant exceeds 64 digits	The SX-Key assembler can not handle constants whose value is larger than 32 bits or 64 digits.
Clock frequency must be from 400_000 to 110_000_000	Designated frequency used in the FREQ directive is outside the range. The SX-Key can only clock the SX chip between 400 KHz and 110 KHz.
ELSE/ENDIF must be preceded by IF	Check for missing or commented-out IF directive above the ELSE/ENDIF.
Empty string	Look for undefined string within quotes.
ENDIF required to end IF block	Check for missing or commented-out ENDIF directive below the IF.
ENDM required to end MACRO definition	Check for missing or commented-out ENDM at the end of a MACRO definition.
ENDR must be preceded by REPT	Check for missing or commented-out REPT directive above the ENDR.
ENDR required to end REPT block	Check for missing or commented-out ENDR directive below the REPT.
EQU must be preceded by a label	A valid symbol must precede the EQU directive. Check for mistyped symbol. Watch out for different case when the CASE directive is used.

Message	Explanation
Error message contains control characters	Error message defined with an ERROR directive must contain printable characters only.
Error message exceeds 64 characters	Error message defined with an ERROR directive must be 64 characters or less in length.
EXITM/ENDM must be preceded by MACRO	Check for missing or commented-out MACRO directive above the EXITM/ENDM.
Expected "++" or "--"	The source operand in a MOVSZ must be preceded by ++ or --.
Expected ","	Check for missing arguments on a multi-argument mnemonic.
Expected "," or end-of-line	Check for invalid character(s) at the end of the line.
Expected a binary operator or ")"	
Expected a constant	
Expected a constant, variable, unary operator, or "("	Look for mnemonic with bad or missing arguments. Look for incomplete expressions.
Expected a DEVICE parameter	DEVICE directive contains a missing or invalid parameter. Look for misspellings, commas without trailing parameters, lower case when using CASE directive, etc.
Expected a label, directive, or instruction	Check for invalid arguments. Check for mistyped mnemonic.
Expected a value from 0 to 64 or end-of-line	Argument count on macros must be 0 to 64 or not specified.
Expected a value from 1 to 32	The count parameter in the WATCH directive must be in the range of 1 to 32.
Expected a terminating quote	Look for a string without a terminating quote, or apostrophe.
Expected an expression	Look for a mnemonic with missing arguments.
Expected end-of-line	Look for invalid character or argument at the end-of-line. Look for incomplete expression.
Expected UDEC, SDEC, UHEX, SHEX, UBIN, SBIN, FSTR or ZSTR	WATCH directive is missing formatter argument.
Expected W	The W argument is missing in a mnemonic that requires it.
Expected WDT	The clear-watchdog mnemonic must specify !WDT
Expression is too complex	SX-Key assembler cannot handle the designated expression. Try simplifying the expression if possible.
ID cannot exceed 8 characters	A maximum of 8 characters are allowed in the ID directive.
ID must be a string of up to 8 characters	Make sure to use single quotes, or apostrophes, ('), before and after the string. Make sure not to input control characters.
Location already contains data	Assembled instruction overlaps used memory or crossed over last defined page barrier. Can also occur when the RESET directive is specified twice.
Label is already defined	A symbol, or label, is already defined or is a reserved word. Make sure label's position is not invalid, such as a label in a REPT block (this would make duplicate labels during the expansion). Make sure label starts with a letter or an underscore (_).
Limit of 32 nested REPTs exceeded	The SX-Key assembler cannot process more than 32 nested REPT blocks.
Limit of 100,000 total REPT loops exceeded	REPT count argument must be in the range 1..100,000.
List is too large	List file generation cannot complete because it is too large. Look for REPT blocks whose count is high, or whose final size, during assembly, is large.
Macro argument index is out of range	The designated argument index is outside the specified range as set by the macro's definition.
Macro argument is not resolvable	
MACRO must be preceded by a label	A valid symbol must precede the MACRO directive. Check for mistyped symbol.

Message	Explanation
Macro stack overflow	Macro is too complex; try simplifying it.
Nothing to assemble	Must have source code entered or loaded up into the editor before assembling, programming, running or debugging.
Only one BREAK is allowed	The SX chip does not support more than one breakpoint at a time.
Port is out of range	Verify the port symbol or address in the mnemonic. See Appendix F for available ports.
Redundant DEVICE parameter	The parameter specified conflicts with a previously specified device parameter.
REPT count must be greater than 0	
RESET address must be on first page	The SX chip does not support a reset address outside of page 0.
Symbol exceeds 32 characters	All symbols must be 32 characters in length or less and must start with a letter or underscore (_).
Symbol table full	Too many symbols are defined. Must limit or combine any applicable symbols to assemble properly.
This directive cannot be preceded by a symbol	Only the ORG, RESET, EQU, =, DS, DW, BREAK, MACRO and END directives can be preceded by a symbol.
Undefined Symbol	Symbol is not defined above highlighted line. Check for mistyped symbol. Watch out for different case when the CASE directive is used.
Unrecognized character	Use single quotes (') instead of double quotes (").
Variable must be followed by "="	Look for mistyped label.

8.7 Data Types

Data types are handled by the Parallax assembler similar to SASM. Therefore, refer to **Chapter 7.8 – Data Types** for more details.

8.8 Reserved Words and Symbols

Table 18 – Parallax Assembler Reserved Words, below, summarizes the words that are reserved in the Parallax assembler, i.e. you may not use any of these words for a symbol or label.

Table 18 - Parallax Assembler Reserved Words

ADD	DRT60MS *	MOV	RB	SZ
ADDB	DRT60US *	MOVB	RC	TEST
AND	DRT960MS *	MOVSZ	RD *	TIMER CAPTURE HIGH *
BANK	DS	NOCASE	RE *	TIMER CAPTURE LOW *
BOR22	DW	NOEXPAND	REPT	TIMER COMPARE1 HIGH *
BOR26	END	NOP	RESET	TIMER COMPARE1 LOW *
BOR42	ENDM	NOT	RET	TIMER COMPARE2 HIGH *
BREAK	ENDR	OPTION	RETI	TIMER COMPARE2 LOW *
C	EQU	OR	RETIW	TIMER CONTROL A *
CALL	ERROR	ORG	RETP	TIMER CONTROL B *
CARRYX	EXITM	OSC128KHZ	RETW	TO
CASE	EXPAND	OSC1MHZ	RL	TRIS
CJA	FEEDBACKOFF	OSC32KHZ	RR	TURBO
CJAE	FREQ	OSC4MHZ	RTCC	UBIN
CJB	FSR	OSCHS1	SB	UDEC
CJBE	FSTR	OSCHS2	SBIN	UHEX
CJE	ID	OSCHS3	SC	W
CJNE	IFBD	OSCLP1	SCHMITT	WAKE EDGE
CLC	IJNZ	OSCLP2	SDEC	WAKE ENABLE
CLR	INC	OSCRC	SET	WAKE PENDING
CLRB	INCSZ	OSCXT1	SETB	WATCH
CLZ	IND	OSCXT2	SHEX	WATCHDOG
CMP	INDF	OSCXT3	SKIP	WDT
COMPARATOR	INDIRECT	OSCXT4	SLEEP	WKED
CSA	IREAD	OSCXT5	SLEEPCLOCK *	WKEN
CSAE	JB	OSCXTMAX	SNB	WKPEN
CSB	JC	OSCXTMIN	SNC	WREG
CSBE	JMP	PA0	SNZ	XOR
CSE	JNB	PA1	ST	XTLBUFD
CSNE	JNC	PA2	STACKX OPTIONX **	Z
DC	JNZ	PAGE	STATUS	ZSTR
DEC	JZ	PC	STC	
DECSZ	LEVEL	PD	STZ	
DIRECTION	LVL	PLP	SUB	
DJNZ	M	PROTECT	SUBB	
DRIVEOFF *	MACRO	PULL UP	SWAP	
DRT18MS *	MODE	RA	SYNC	

* = SX48/52 only, ** = SX 20/28 only

9 Upgrading Existing Code for SASM

This chapter describes the most common changes that need to be made to use existing code for the Parallax Assembler with the SASM assembler.

- Add an IRC_CAL directive to all existing projects, usually below the DEVICE directives to avoid the "no IRC_CAL" warning. If you don't intend to use the internal RC oscillator, use the IRC_SLOW or IRC_FAST rather than the IRC_4MHZ option. The IRC_4MHZ option always increases the download time since the SX-Key needs to run special calibration routines.
- Add a FREQ directive to all existing projects to avoid the "no FREQ" warning.
- Replace STACKX_OPTIONX by either STACKX or OPTIONX in projects for SX20 or SX28 devices. No matter which directive you use, both the stack and the option register will be extended to 8-bits; there is no need to specify both. For SX48/52 devices use of STACKX or OPTIONX will cause a warning because these devices have these options always on by default.
- Replace FEEDBACKOFF with IFBD when used in the source code.
- Replace SLEEPCLOCK with SLEEPCLK when used in source code for the SX48/52.
- Replace DRT18MS with WDRT184, DRT960MS with WDRT960, DRT60MS with WDRT60, and DRT60US with WDRT006 when used in source code for the SX48/52.
- Add a LIST Q = 37 directive at the beginning if the source code to suppress "Literal truncated…" warnings.
- Modify any user-defined words that are reserved words in SASM.
- Add equates for Parallax reserved words that are not reserved in SASM if necessary.
- *Add an OSCxxx directive to each project when there is none in the original code. SASM assumes OSCRC by default where the Parallax Assembler assumes an OSCHS2 instead. The SASM assembler will issue a warning message when it does not find an OSCxxx directive in the source code.*

10 SX Special Features and Coding Tips

10.1 Introduction

The SX chip offers many configurable features. This chapter explains how to use many of these features, offers coding tips and demonstrates most topics with sample code. All examples are written for the SX20/28 chips and may need modification for SX48/52 chips.

10.2 Port Configuration and Usage

There are many configuration options for each of the ports on the SX chip as shown in **Table 19 – Port Configuration Options**, below. The following sections explain how to use the various port configuration options.

Table 19 - Port Configuration Options

Type	Port A	Port B	Port C*	Port D*	Port E*
Input/Output	X	X	X	X	X
Pull-Ups	X	X	X	X	X
CMOS/TTL	X	X	X	X	X
Schmitt-Trigger		X	X	X	X
Edge-Interrupts		X			
Comparator		Three Pins			

* Port C not available on SX20, Port D and E only available on SX48/52 devices.

To set these functions, a special form of the MOV instruction, called the port configuration instruction, is used to modify the port configuration registers. The syntax of this instruction is:

```
MOV        !port, src
```

By default, the port configuration instruction writes to the port direction registers, called the tristate registers. To write to other registers, the MODE register must be preset with a specific value. **Table 20 – MODE Register Settings** lists these values. See chapter **15.4.1 – MODE Register** for more information.

Table 20 - MODE Register Settings

MODE	Port A	Port B	Port C*	Port D*	Port E*
$0F	' RIS_A	TRIS_B	TRIS_C	TRIS_D	TRIS_E
$0E	PLP_A	PLP_B	PLP_C	PLP_D	PLP_E
$0D	LVL_A	LVL_B	LVL_C	LVL_D	LVL_E
$0C		ST_B	ST_C	ST_D	ST_E
$0B		WKEN_B			
$0A		WKED_B			
$09		Swap W with WKPEN_B			
$08		Swap W with COMP_B			
$07 - $00					

* Port C not available on SX20 devices, Port D and E only available on SX48/52 devices.
NOTE: More options exist for the SX48/52 parts. See chapter 15.4.2 for details.

10.2.1 Port Direction

Each of the I/O pins in each of the ports can be configured to an input or output direction by writing to the appropriate tristate register (TRIS_A, TRIS_B, TRIS_C, TRIS_D and TRIS_E). The default I/O pin direction is input. I/O pin direction configuration is usually done once, near the start of code, however, the pin directions can be changed multiple times at any place in the code.

To configure the direction of the I/O pins to inputs or outputs:

1) Set the MODE register to $0F (the default value at startup).
2) Use the port configuration instruction to set the individual directions of each I/O pin within each port. A high bit (1) sets the corresponding pin to input mode and a low bit (0) sets the pin to output mode.

The following code snippet demonstrates this:

```
; Direction Configuration
;
MODE  $0F              ; Set Mode to allow Direction configuration
MOV   !ra,#%0000       ; Port A bits 0-3 to output
MOV   !rb,#%11110000   ; Port B bits 4-7 to input, bits 0-3 output
MOV   !rc,#%00001111   ; Port C bits 4-7 to output, bits 0-3 input
```

If the logic-level of output pins are expected to begin at a certain state (0 or 1), care should be taken to set the output latch appropriately before setting the pin's direction to output. Failing to do so may result in a momentary glitch on the pin during initialization. For example, if all output pins were expected to begin in a low state (0), insert the following lines above the previous code snippet:

```
; Set output pins low
;
MOV     ra, #%0000        ; Port A bits 0-3 low
MOV     rb, #%00000000    ; Port B bits 0-7 low
MOV     rc, #%00000000    ; Port C bits 0-7 low
```

10.2.2 Pull-Up Resistors

Every I/O pin has optional internal pull-up resisters that can be configured by writing to the appropriate pull-up register (PLP_A, PLP_B, PLP_C, PLP_D and PLP_E). By configuring pull-up resisters on input pins, the SX chip can be connected directly to open/drain circuitry without the need for external pull-up resisters. The internal pull-up resisters are disabled by default. Pull-up resisters can be activated for all pins, regardless of pin direction but really matter only when the associated pin is set to input mode.

To configure the I/O pins to have internal pull-up resisters:

1) Set the MODE register to $0E (the value for pull-up register configuration).
2) Use the port configuration instruction to set the individual pull-up state of each I/O pin within each port. A high bit (1) disables the pull-up for the corresponding pin and a low bit (0) enables the pull-up resister for a pin.
3) Set I/O pin directions as necessary.

The following code snippet demonstrates this:

```
; Pull-Up Resistor Configuration
;
MODE   $0E                ; Set Mode for Pull-Up Resistor configuration
MOV    !ra,#%0000         ; Port A bits 0-3 to pull-ups
MOV    !rb,#%11110000     ; Port B bits 4-7 normal, bits 0-3 pull-ups
MOV    !rc,#%00001111     ; Port C bits 4-7 pull-ups, bits 0-3 normal
MODE   $0F                ; Set Mode to allow Direction configuration
MOV    !ra,#%1111         ; Port A bits 0-3 to input
MOV    !rb,#%00001111     ; Port B bits 4-7 to output, bits 0-3 input
MOV    !rc,#%11110000     ; Port C bits 4-7 to input, bits 0-3 output
```

10.2.3 Logic Level

Every I/O pin has selectable logic level control that determines the voltage threshold for a logic level 0 or 1. The default logic level for all I/O pins is TTL but can be modified by writing to the appropriate logic-level register (LVL_A, LVL_B, LVL_C, LVL_D and LVL_E). The logic level can be configured for all pins, regardless of pin direction, but really matters only when the associated pin is set to input mode. By configuring logic levels on input pins, the SX chip can be sensitive to both TTL and CMOS logic thresholds. **Figure 14 – TTL and CMOS Levels**, below, demonstrates the difference between TTL and CMOS logic levels.

Figure 14 - TTL and CMOS Levels

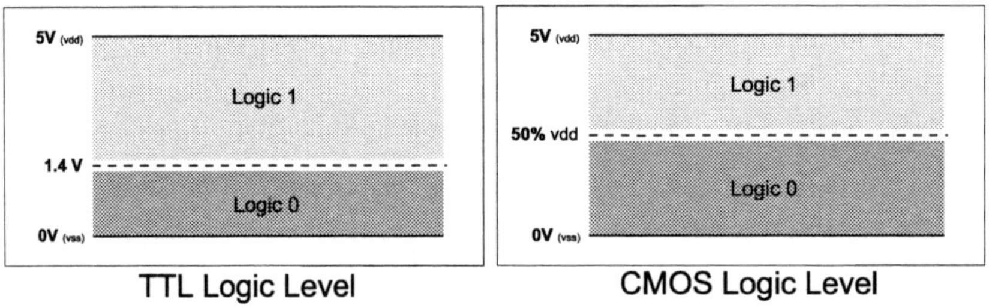

The logic threshold for TTL is 1.4 volts; a voltage below 1.4 is considered to be a logic 0, while a voltage above is considered to be a logic 1. The logic threshold for CMOS is 50% of Vdd, a voltage below ½ Vdd is considered to be a logic 0, while a voltage above ½ Vdd is considered to be a logic 1.

To configure the I/O pins to use CMOS- or TTL-level logic:

1) Set the MODE register to $0D (the value for logic-level register configuration).

2) Use the port configuration instruction to set the individual logic-level state of each I/O pin within each port. A high bit (1) sets the corresponding pin to TTL-level logic and a low bit (0) sets it to CMOS-level logic.

3) Set I/O pin directions as necessary.

The following code snippet demonstrates this:

```
; Logic Level Configuration
;
MODE  $0D            ; Set Mode to Logic Level configuration
MOV   !ra,#%0000     ; Port A bits 0-3 to CMOS
MOV   !rb,#%11110000 ; Port B bits 4-7 to TTL, bits 0-3 CMOS
MOV   !rc,#%00001111 ; Port C bits 4-7 to CMOS, bits 0-3 TTL
MODE  $0F            ; Set Mode to allow Direction configuration
MOV   !ra,#%1100     ; Port A bits 0-1 to output, bits 2-3 input
MOV   !rb,#%10110011 ; Port B bits 2,3,6 to output, all others input
MOV   !rc,#%11011110 ; Port C bits 0,5 to output, all others input
```

10.2.4 Schmitt-Trigger

Every I/O pin in port B through port E can be set to normal or Schmitt-Trigger input. This can be configured by writing to the appropriate Schmitt-Trigger register (ST_B, ST_C, ST_D and ST_E). The I/O pins are set to normal input mode by default. Schmitt-Trigger mode can be activated for all pins, regardless of pin direction but really matter only when the associated pin is set to input mode. By configuring Schmitt-Trigger mode on input pins, the SX chip can be less sensitive to minor noise on the input pins. , below, details the characteristics of Schmitt-Trigger inputs.

Figure 15 - Schmitt Trigger Characteristics

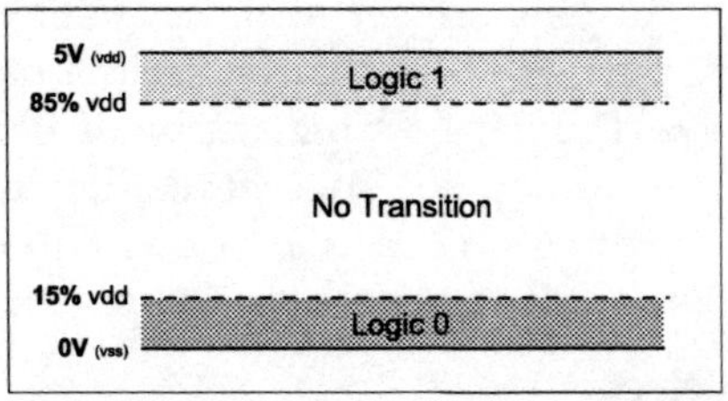

Schmitt-Trigger inputs are conditioned with a large area of hysteresis. The threshold for a logic 0 is 15% of Vdd and the threshold for a logic 1 is 85% of Vdd. The input pin defaults to an unknown state until the initial voltage crosses a logic 0 or logic 1 boundary. A voltage must cross above 85% of Vdd to be interpreted as a logic 1 and must cross below 15% of Vdd to be interpreted as a logic 0. If the voltage transitions somewhere between the two thresholds, the interpreted logic state remains the same as the previous state.

To configure the I/O pins to Schmitt-Trigger input:

1) Set the MODE register to $0C (the value for Schmitt-Trigger register configuration).
2) Use the port configuration instruction to set the individual Schmitt-Trigger state of each I/O pin within each port. A high bit (1) sets the corresponding pin to normal and a low bit (0) sets it to Schmitt-Trigger.
3) Set I/O pin directions as necessary.

The following code snippet demonstrates this:

```
; Schmitt-Trigger Configuration
;
MODE   $0C               ; Set Mode to Schmitt Trigger configuration
MOV    !rb,#%11110000  ; Port B bits 4-7 to normal, bits 0-3 to S.T.
MOV    !rc,#%00001111  ; Port C bits 4-7 to S.T., bits 0-3 normal
MODE   $0F               ; Set Mode to allow Direction configuration
MOV    !rb,#%10110011  ; Port B bits 2,3,6 to output, all others input
MOV    !rc,#%11011110  ; Port C bits 0,5 to output, all others input
```

10.2.5 Edge Detection

Every I/O pin in port B can be set to detect logic level transitions (rising edge or falling edge). This can be configured by writing to the Edge Selection register (WKED_B) and detected by monitoring the Pending register (WKPEN_B). The I/O pins are set to detect falling edge transitions by default. By configuring edge detection on input pins, the SX chip can set the pin's associated bit in the Pending register when the desired edge arrives. The Pending register bits will never be cleared by the SX alone; the running program is responsible for doing so. This means, if a desired edge is detected, the flag indicating this will remain set until the program has time to attend to it. This feature can be used by the SX program for signals that need attention, but not necessarily immediately.

To configure the I/O pins for edge detection:

1) Set the MODE register to $0A (the value for Edge Detect register configuration).
2) Use the port configuration instruction to set the individual edge to detect on each I/O pin. A high bit (1) sets the corresponding pin to falling-edge detection and a low bit (0) sets it to rising-edge detection.
3) Set I/O pin directions as necessary.

The following code snippet demonstrates this:

```
        ; Edge Detection Configuration
        ;
Start
        MODE   $0A                 ; Set Mode to allow Edge configuration
        MOV    !rb,#%11111111      ; Port B bits 0-7 to falling edge
        MODE   $0F                 ; Set Mode to allow Direction configuration
        MOV    !rb,#%11111111      ; Port B bits 0-7 to input

Main
        MODE   $09                 ; Set Mode for Pending register check
        MOV    !rb,#%00000000      ; This line moves WKPND_B to W and
                                   ; writes all zeros to WKPND_B
        JMP    Main                ; At this point, W should be checked for
                                   ; high bits, indicating a falling
                                   ; edge occurred
```

The following are points to remember with edge detection:

- The edge detection feature is always enabled and the Pending register is always updated even if the SX program does not configure or use it.
- It is up to the SX program to clear the bits of the Pending register when detection of a future transition is desired. The MOV !rb, #%00000000 instruction effectively clears all bits of the Pending register at the same time that it stores the current edge detection status in W.
- If the SX program is designed to handle only one edge detection event at a time (on two or more pins), it will be necessary to get the status (as shown above), clear only the bit being attended to and move the modified status back to the Pending register.
- An edge detection event will not wake up the SX chip from a SLEEP mode unless the Wake-Up Enable mode is also set. See below for more information.

10.2.6 Wakeup (Interrupt) on Edge Detection

Every I/O pin in port B can be set to cause an interrupt upon logic level transitions (rising edge or falling edge). By configuring interrupts on input pins, the SX chip can respond to signal changes in a quick and deterministic fashion. In addition, an interrupt of this sort will wake up the SX chip from a SLEEP state. This can be configured by writing to the Edge Selection register (WKED_B) and the Wake-Up Enable register (WKEN_B) and detected by monitoring the Pending register (WKPEN_B) in the interrupt routine. The I/O pins have interrupts disabled and are set to detect falling edge transitions by default.

As with edge selection, the Pending register bits will never be cleared by the SX alone; the running program is responsible for doing so. This means if a desired edge is detected, the interrupt will occur and the flag indicating this will remain set until the program clears it. Additional transitions on that pin will not cause interrupts until the associated bit in the Pending register is cleared.

To configure the I/O pins for wake-up (interrupt) edge detection:

1) Set I/O pin edge detection as desired. (See Edge Detection, above, for more information).
2) Set the MODE register to $0B (the value for Wake-Up Enable register configuration).
3) Use the port configuration instruction to enable the individual pins for wake-up interrupts. A high bit (1) disables interrupts and a low bit (0) enables interrupts.
4) Set I/O pin directions as necessary.
5) Clear the Pending register to enable new interrupts.

The following code snippet demonstrates this:

```
        RESET  Start

Interrupt                           ; Interrupt routine (must be at address $0)
        ORG    $0
        MODE   $09                  ; Set Mode for Pending register
        MOV    !rb,%00000000        ; Clear Pending/get current status in W
        RETI                        ; rest of interrupt routine goes here

        ; Wake-Up Edge Detection Configuration
        ;
Start
        MODE   $0A                  ; Set Mode to allow Edge configuration
        MOV    !rb,#%11111111       ; Port B bits 0-7 to falling edge
        MODE   $0B                  ; Set Mode to allow Wake-Up configuration
        MOV    !rb#%11110000        ; Port B bits 4-7 to normal, 0-3 to Wake-Up
        MODE   $0F                  ; Set Mode to allow Direction configuration
        MOV    !rb,#%11111111       ; Port B bits 0-7 to input
        MODE   $09                  ; Set Mode for Pending register
        MOV    !rb,%00000000        ; Clear register to allow new interrupts
Main
        NOP                         ; rest of main routine goes here
        JMP    Main
```

The following are points to remember with Wake-Up Interrupts:

- The interrupt routine must be located starting at address $0 in the SX program.
- It is up to the SX program to clear the bits of the Pending register when future interrupts on that pin are desired. This should normally be done as part of the interrupt routine. The MOV !rb, #%00000000 instruction effectively clears all bits of the Pending register at the same time that it stores the current edge detection status in W.
- The SX chip will activate the interrupt routine exactly 5 clock cycles in Turbo mode or exactly 10 clock cycles in compatible mode after a Wake-Up Edge Detection event occurs. This deterministic feature allows for nearly jitter-free interrupt response. Latency may vary by as much as +1 instruction cycle when interrupting on external asynchronous events, thus a high clock speed may be necessary to lessen the effects.
- If multiple interrupt pins are required, the SX chip may not be able to properly process them in certain situations. See Interrupts, below, for more information.
- An edge-detection interrupt event will wake up the SX chip from a SLEEP mode.

10.2.7 Comparator

I/O pins 0 through 2 in port B can be set for comparator operation. This can be configured by writing to the EN and OE bits of the Comparator register (CMP_B) and monitored by reading the RES bit. The comparator mode is disabled by default. Comparator mode can be activated for all three pins, regardless of pin direction, but really matters only when pin 1 and 2 are set to input mode (pin 0 can optionally be set to output the comparative result). By configuring Comparator mode, the SX chip can quickly determine logical differences between two signals and even indicate those differences for external circuitry.

When comparator mode is activated, the RES bit in the Comparator register indicates the result of the compare. A high bit (1) indicates the voltage on pin 2 is higher than that of pin 1, a low bit (0) indicates the voltage on pin 2 is lower than that of pin 1. If the OE bit (Output Enable) of the Comparator register is cleared, output pin 0 of port B reflects the state of the RES bit.

To configure port B I/O pins 0 though 2 for Comparator mode:

1) Set the MODE register to $08 (the value for Comparator register configuration).
2) Use the port configuration instruction to enable the Comparator and, optionally, the result output on pin 0.
3) Set I/O pin directions appropriately.

The following code snippet demonstrates this:

```
        ; Comparator Configuration
        ;
        MODE   $08              ; Set Mode to Comparator configuration
        MOV    !rb,#%00000000   ; Enable comparator and result output
        MODE   $0F              ; Set Mode to allow Direction configuration
        MOV    !rb,#%11111110   ; Port B bits 1-7  to input, bit 0 to input
Main
        MODE   $08
        MOV    !rb,#$00
        JMP    Main             ; Here, bit 0 of W holds result of compare
```

The following are points to remember with Comparator mode:

- Port B I/O pins 1 and 2 are the comparator inputs and I/O pin 0 is, optionally, the comparator result output.
- Port B I/O pin 0 may be used as a normal I/O pin by setting the OE bit of the Comparator register.
- The comparator is independent of the clock source and thus will operate even if the SX chip is halted or in SLEEP mode. To avoid spurious current draw during SLEEP mode, disable the comparator.

10.3 The SX48/52 Multi-Function Timers

In addition to the standard timers (RTCC and watchdog), the SX48/52 devices come with two Multi-Function Timers T1 and T2. These timers are useful to replace a software solution for generating PWM signals, counting events, and generating longer time delays.

Each timer comes with a free-running 16-bit counter. At reset, the counters are initialized with $0000, and then, they start continuously counting upwards. The counters can either be clocked from the system clock (through an 8-bit prescaler), or from an external transition at the external clock pin. This input can be configured to sense positive, or negative transitions.

Each counter has associated 16-bit capture and comparison registers. As an option, various events can be used to trigger an interrupt, or to generate an output signal.

The block diagram in Figure 16 – **SX48/52 Multi-Function Timers**, below, shows the components of one timer:

Figure 16 - SX48/52 Multi-Function Timers

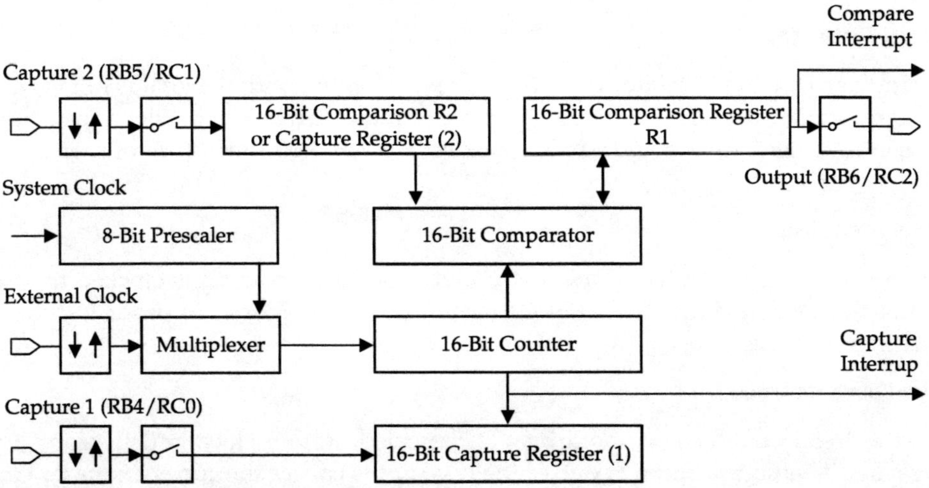

Registers R1, R2 and the capture registers can be accessed by **mov !rb, w** (Timer1), or **mov !rc, w** (Timer2) instructions. The remaining registers cannot be accessed via software.

Timer 1 shares its input and output lines with the Port B pins 4...7, and Timer 2 shares its input and output lines with the Port C pins 0...3. If a timer is active, those pins can no longer used for "regular" I/O purposes.

10.3.1 PWM Mode

In this mode, the timer generates a square wave signal with programmable frequency, and duty cycle. For this purpose, the contents of the two comparison registers determine for how long the signal is high, and low.

The 16-bit counter starts with a value of 0, and keeps incrementing until it has reached the value of R1. Then, the counter is reset to 0, the output is toggled, and (if enabled) an interrupt is generated.

Next, the counter keeps incrementing until it reaches the value of R2. Again, the counter is reset to 0, the output signal is toggled, and an interrupt is triggered (if enabled).

These two steps are repeated continuously. The contents of R1 and R2 determine the frequency and the duty cycle of the generated output signal. When R1 and R2 contain the same value, a square wave with a duty cycle of 50% is generated. In order to generate a signal with a constant frequency, and a varying duty cycle, the sum R1+R2 must remain constant, i.e. to change the duty cycle, increase the value of one register, and decrease the value of the other register by the same amount.

In PWM mode, the 16-bit counter is clocked through the prescaler from the system clock. The prescaler can be set to divide-by factors from 1 to 256 in steps of powers of two.

10.3.2 Software Timer Mode

This mode is similar to the PWM mode with the difference that the output signal is not toggled. Instead, the application program must react on the interrupts that indicate a match between the counter and R1, or between the counter and R2. An additional interrupt is generated when the counter overflows from $ffff to $0000.

10.3.3 External Event Counter

Again, this mode is similar to the PWM mode, but here, the 16-bit counter is clocked from an external signal instead of the system clock. The external input can be configured in order to have positive or negative transitions increment the counter.

10.3.4 Capture/Compare Mode

In this mode, the 16-bit counter is clocked by the prescaled system clock and it keeps incrementing without being reset. A valid transition at one of the two inputs causes the current counter contents to be stored in the associated capture register. This makes it easy to determine the time difference between two external events.

In addition, the counter contents are continuously compared against the contents of register R1. If both are equal, an interrupt is generated (if enabled), and the output signal is toggled. Unlike the PWM mode, the counter is not reset in this case, it keeps incrementing.

In order to obtain a fixed period between the interrupts and output toggles, the ISR must load a new value into R1 whenever an interrupt is triggered.

The two inputs Capture 1 and Capture 2, can be configured to trigger on positive or negative transitions.

Capture register 1 is a separate register dedicated to capture the counter contents only, where Register R2 is used for the capture register 2.

As an option, each capture event can also issue an interrupt and various flags allow the ISR to determine the cause of the interrupt.

In addition, a 16-bit counter overflow can also trigger an interrupt, and set a flag. This is important when the time between two external events is long enough to allow for one or more counter overflows. If the ISR keeps track of the number of overflows, it is possible to calculate the time elapsed between two external events.

10.4 All About Interrupts

The SX20/28 chip allows for up to nine sources of interrupts; eight external and one internal. The SX48/52 chip allows for up to 17 sources of interrupts; 10 external and one internal. Any or all of the port B I/O pins can be configured as external interrupts. See **Chapter 10.2.6 – Wakeup (Interrupt) on Edge Detection** for information on configuring external interrupts. The internal interrupt can be configured to occur upon a rollover condition within the Real Time Clock Counter (RTCC) register. A special return-from-interrupt command may also be used to adjust the value of the RTCC to cause interrupts to occur at a specific time interval. See section 10.4.1 for more information.

In addition to the interrupts supported by the SX20/28, with the SX48/52 devices, six different internal interrupts can be configured for the Timer 1 and Timer 2 overflow and R1/R2 counter comparison registers.

These interrupt options can be very powerful features but can also cause havoc if not configured or understood properly. If using interrupts of any kind is desired, the following items should be reviewed.

- *Interrupt Vector:* The interrupt vector in the SX chip points to address $0 and is not configurable. The interrupt routine must reside at location $0 to be properly executed upon an interrupt event.
- *Auto Interrupt Disable:* As soon as an interrupt occurs, additional interrupts are automatically ignored by the SX chip until the interrupt routine is completed. This prevents the interrupt routine from being interrupted and prevents the loss of return vector data. This is also one of the most important considerations when working with interrupts; you can not immediately (without jitter) process more than one interrupt at a time.

  Note: Should additional interrupts occur, the SX chip does not automatically queue up interrupts for future processing. See Interrupt Queuing, below, for more information.
- *Latency Delays:* When an interrupt occurs, there is a latency delay before the interrupt routine is actually activated. For the internal RTCC rollover, this latency is exactly 3 clock cycles in Turbo mode and 8 clock cycles in Compatible mode. For the external interrupts, the latency delay is exactly 5 clock cycles in Turbo mode and 10 clock cycles in Compatible mode. Latency may vary by as much as +1 instruction cycle when interrupting on external asynchronous events, thus a high clock speed may be necessary to lessen the effects.
- *Interrupt Routine Size:* Normally it is a requirement for an application to process every interrupt without missing any. To ensure this happens, the longest path through the interrupt routine must take less time than the shortest possible delay between interrupts.
- *Interrupt Queuing:* If an external interrupt occurs during the interrupt routine, the pending register will be updated but the trigger will be ignored unless interrupts had first been turned off at the beginning of the routine and turned on again at the end. This also requires that the new interrupt doesn't occur before interrupts are turned off in the interrupt routine. If there is a possibility of extra interrupts occurring before they can be disabled, the SX will miss those interrupt triggers.

- *Multiple Interrupts:* Using more than one interrupt, such as multiple external interrupts or both RTCC and external interrupts, can result in missed or, at best, jittery interrupt handling should one occur during the processing of another.
- *Clearing Pending Bits:* When handling external interrupts, the interrupt routine should clear at least one pending register bit. The bit that is cleared should represent the interrupt being handled in order for the next interrupt to trigger.
- *Debugging Interrupts:* The SX chip may act strangely while debugging code that contains interrupts. The SX chip may or may not enter the RTCC interrupt routine (and will never enter a MIWU interrupt) while using the Step or Walk functions. This is due to the SX chip giving higher priority to the SX-Key than its internal interrupt flags. *If interrupt code needs to be debugged or verified, place a BREAK directive, or a breakpoint, in an appropriate place within the interrupt routine and use the Run or Poll functions.*

10.4.1 RTCC Rollover Interrupts

The SX chip can be set to cause an interrupt upon rollover of the Real Time Clock Counter (RTCC). By configuring an interrupt on RTCC rollover, the SX chip can perform an operation at a predefined time interval in a deterministic fashion. This can be configured by setting the STACKX or OPTIONX fuse (in the DEVICE directive) and writing to the RTI, RTS and RTE bits of the Option register (OPTION). The RTCC rollover interrupt is disabled by default.

To configure the RTCC rollover interrupt:

1) Set the STACKX or OPTIONX fuse in the DEVICE line.
2) Write to the RTI, RTS and RTE bits of the OPTION register to enable RTCC interrupts. For RTI, a high bit (1) disables RTCC rollover interrupts and a low bit (0) enables RTCC rollover interrupts. For RTS, a high bit (1) selects incrementing RTCC on internal clock cycle and a low bit (0) increments RTCC on the RTCC pin transitions. For RTE, a high bit (1) selects incrementing on low-to-high transition and a low bit (0) increments on a high-to-low transition.

The following code snippet demonstrates this:

```
        DEVICE STACKX
        RESET  Start

        ORG    $0

Interrupt                             ; Interrupt routine (must be at address $0)
        RETI                          ; rest of interrupt routine goes here

        ; RTCC Rollover Interrupt Configuration
        ;
Start
        MOV    !OPTION, #%10011111    ; Enable RTCC rollover interrupt
                                      ; RTCC inc on clock, no prescale
Main
        NOP                           ; rest of main routine goes here
        JMP    Main
```

The above code will cause the interrupt routine to be executed once every 256 clock cycles (when RTCC rolls over from 255 to 0). A different return-from-interrupt command called RETIW can be used, however, to customize the time interval (cycle interval) in which the interrupt executes. RETIW, like RETI, causes a return from the interrupt routine. RETIW has the additional effect of adding the contents of W to the RTCC register upon return. By moving a negative number into W just before executing an RETIW, the RTCC will be backed-off by the designated number of cycles. This method also has the benefit of compensating for the number of cycles spent in the interrupt routine.

For example, if the interrupt routine should be executed once every 50 cycles, use the following two lines of code in place of the RETI command in the listing above:

```
        MOV    W, #-50
        RETIW
```

Of course, for this to work properly the interrupt routine must take 46 cycles or less (see below for cycle bandwidth calculation). Even if the interrupt routine contained multiple paths of execution, due to compare-jump instructions, and each path consumed a different number of clock cycles, the interrupt would still execute once every 50 cycles. **Table 21 – Interrupt Timing**, below, demonstrates the effects on the RTCC if the interrupt routine contained two possible paths of execution (path 1 is 28 cycles and path 2 is 15 cycles):

Table 21 - Interrupt Timing

Event	Path 1 (28 cycles)	Path 2 (15 cycles)
1) RTCC rolls over	RTCC = 0	RTCC = 0
2) 3 cycles required to enter interrupt routine	RTCC = 3	RTCC = 3
3) Interrupt routine executes	RTCC = 31	RTCC = 18
4) –50 (206 in twos-compliment) is added to RTCC	RTCC = 237	RTCC = 224
5) RTCC rolls over again in exactly 19 additional cycles (Path 1) or 32 additional cycles (Path 2)	Total Cycles = 31 + 19 = 50	Total Cycles = 18 + 32 = 50

By adjusting the value in W before the RETIW command, various amounts of cycle bandwidth will be allocated to the main routines. Normally this won't be a problem but care should be taken to ensure that the RTCC doesn't rollover too often, causing little or no cycle time to be allocated to the main routines. If the RTCC adjustment value is too small for the size of the interrupt routine, the main routine may eventually hang up, may not execute at all, or the interrupt routine will miss the rollover and only execute every 256 cycles. Use the following equation as a general rule-of-thumb when determining the minimum adjustment value:

Minimum RTCC Adjustment Value = -(max cycles for interrupt + 6)

The 6 in this equation accounts for the number of cycles required to enter the interrupt routine (3 cycles) plus the number of additional cycles needed to complete the longest command (3 cycles extra to finish an IREAD). If the IREAD command is not used in the main program, a value of -(maximum cycles for interrupt + 4) is the minimum, allowing for only a single instruction in the main routine to be executed between interrupts.

As an example, the following interrupt routine takes 4 cycles to execute:

```
Interrupt
        MOV    W, #-8             ; 1 cycle
        RETIW                     ; 3 cycles
```

The adjustment value of –8, which is –(max cycles for interrupt + 4), will cause the interrupt routine to execute every 8 cycles and will only allow one single-cycle or one three-cycle instruction in the main routine to execute between interrupts. If the main routine contained an IREAD command, however, the main routine would execute one instruction between interrupts until it reached the IREAD, at which point it would get eternally stuck, and only the interrupt would continue. As another example, if the adjustment value was –7, this would be too small an adjustment and would cause the interrupt routine to execute, but no instructions in the main routine would execute at all.

The following are points to remember with Wake-Up Interrupts:

- The interrupt routine must be located starting at address $0 in the SX program.
- The interrupt routine should take a maximum of 6 cycles less than the desired cycle time slot. (i.e. if the interrupt should execute once every 20 cycles, it needs to be less than 15 cycles in size).
- The SX chip will activate the interrupt routine exactly 3 clock cycles (Turbo) or 8 clock cycles (Compatible) after an RTCC rollover event occurs. This deterministic feature allows for jitter-free interrupt response.

An RTCC rollover interrupt event will not occur during SLEEP mode and thus can not wake up the SX chip from a SLEEP mode.

10.5 Creating Tables

10.5.1 Data Tables

Tables of 8-bit or 12-bit data may be stored in the unused program space of the SX chip. Tables of data may be necessary in cases where a set of data can not be calculated by an equation, or will take too long to calculate. There are two methods available to store data tables in the SX chip.

If only 8-bit data is required, the RETW method may be used to create the data table. This method uses a set of RETW commands which each hold an 8-bit data value as their operand. The table is preceded by a JMP PC+W command. By moving an index value to W and then CALLing the first line of the table, which is the JMP command, W is added to the program counter and upon the next clock cycle, the proper RETW command is executed. RETW simply moves its operand to W and then returns to the line after the CALL.

To create an 8-bit data table with the RETW command:

1) Set the table's location, and insert a label and a JMP PC+W command at the start of the table.
2) Add as many RETW commands as necessary.
3) When data is needed from the table, move the index value of the desired item to W and CALL the table. Upon returning, the 8-bit value is in W.

The following code snippet demonstrates this:

```
        RESET   Main

        Idx     EQU $08             ; Define index symbol

        ; 8-bit data table
        ;
        ORG     $0
Table
        JMP     PC+W                ; Jump into the table
        RETW    'ABCDEFG'           ; Store text
        RETW    10, 100, 255, 0     ; Store numbers

Main
        MOV     Idx, #$FF           ; Reset table index

MainLoop
        INC     Idx                 ; Increment table index
        MOV     W, Idx
        CALL    Table               ; Retrieve data
```

If 8-bit or 12-bit data is required, the DW method may be used to create the data table. This method uses a set of DW (Define Word) directives each of which place a 12-bit data value in program memory. By moving a 12-bit index value to M and W (upper 4 bits of address in M) and executing an IREAD command, M and W are replaced with the 12-bit data value.

To create an 8-bit or 12-bit data table with the DW directive:

1) Set the table's location and insert a label.
2) Add as many DW directives as necessary.

When data is needed from the table, move the index value of the desired item (in relation to the label) to M and W and execute an IREAD. Upon returning, the 12-bit value is in M and W.

The following code snippet demonstrates this:

```
        RESET  Main

        Idx    EQU $08         ; Define index symbol

        ; 8-bit data table
        ,
        ORG    $0
Table   DW     'ABCDEFG'       ; Store text
        DW     10, 300, 4095, 0 ; Store numbers

Main
        MOV    Idx, #Table     ; Reset table index

MainLoop
        MOV    M, #Table>>8    ; upper 4-bits of table address
        MOV    W, Idx          ; lower 8-bits of table index
        IREAD                  ; Retrieve data
;       {use the data}
        INC    Idx             ; Increment table index
        CJNE   Idx, #11, Main  ; Continue
```

Both table methods shown above will only access a maximum of 256 elements, however, the DW method can easily be modified to access every possible address. If speed is desired, the DW method, above, is 4 cycles shorter per element than the RETW method.

10.6 Dealing with Code Pages

10.6.1 Branching Across Pages

The SX chip's program memory is organized into pages of 512 words each. If a program won't fit within a single page, special care must be taken when branching across page boundaries to avoid misdirected jumps.

All instructions that perform a jump, except JMP W, JMP and PC+W, use a 9-bit address as the operand. This limits the jump range to the current page only (512 words). To jump across a page boundary, the page select bits (the upper bits of the Status register) must first be set to the appropriate page before executing the jump. The SX assembler provides a convenient method of doing this, as shown below.

To jump across page boundaries:

Specify the jump command (JMP, JB, CJE, etc) with the page-set option (the @ sign preceding the address).

The following code snippet demonstrates this:

```
Start       ORG $0        ; This routine is in page 0
            JMP  @Routine; Jump to proper page
            JMP  Start

Routine     ORG $200      ; This routine is in page 1
            JMP  @Start   ; Jump back to proper page
```

The @ symbol preceding the address causes the assembler to insert a PAGE instruction just before the JMP to set the page select bits appropriately. The second JMP in line three does not require an @ symbol since the destination address is within the current page. If the @ was left out of line two, the SX would jump to address $000 instead of $200. See **Chapter 15.2.14 - Jumping Across Pages** for more information.

10.6.2 Calling Across Pages with Jump Tables

Calling subroutines can pose even more boundary problems than jumping across pages. The CALL instruction uses only an 8-bit address as the operand (the 9th bit of the address is always cleared). This limits the calling destination to the first 256 words of the current page.

Because it is sometimes impossible to organize all subroutines within such a tight space, a common practice is to make use of a subroutine jump table. The jump table consists of a list of JMP commands to various subroutines and is located within the first 256 words of the page. The CALL instructions can simply call the proper location within the jump table and code execution jumps to the appropriate subroutine, even if it exists in different pages or above the 256 word barrier.

To call subroutines across page boundaries:

1) Design a jump table with the page-set option (the @ sign preceding the addresses).
2) Place the subroutines in any desired location being sure to end them with RETP.
3) Call the subroutine's alias-name in the jump table.

The following code snippet demonstrates this:

```
            ORG         $0          ; This routine is in page 0

            ; Define the subroutine jump-table
            ;
Sub1        JMP         @_Sub1      ; Set page and jump
Sub2        JMP         @_Sub2

            ; Start of main routines
            ;
Start       CALL        @Sub1       ; Call the Jump Table
            JMP         @Continue

            ORG         $200        ; This routine is in page 1

Continue
            CALL        @Sub2       ; Call the Jump Table
            JMP         @Start

            ORG         $400        ; This routine is in page 2
_Sub1       ; Subroutine 1 code goes here
            ;
            RETP                    ; Return and reset page

_Sub2       ; Subroutine 2 code goes here
            ;
            RETP                    ; Return and reset page
```

The first CALL in the Start routine calls the *Sub1* address in the jump table. The JMP command at *Sub1* then jumps to the *_Sub1* subroutine (in page 2) which eventually returns to the line following the CALL. The RETP command used to return from the subroutine resets the page select bits to the page of the calling routine (exactly as intended).

The @ symbol preceding the addresses causes the SX editor to insert a PAGE instruction just before the JMP and CALL commands to set the page select bits appropriately. The first CALL, in the Start routine, would function the same without an @ symbol, as shown above, since the destination address is within the current page. See **Chapter 15.2.16 – Calling Across Pages** for more information.

11 Appendix A: SX Features

11.1 Introduction

The SX chip is a fully static CMOS MPU conservatively rated for DC to 50 (or 75) MHz operation. The SX provides 2K words of on-chip E^2Flash program memory (4K words in SX48/52). In Turbo mode, all instructions are single cycle except program branches, which take three cycles, and IREAD, which takes four cycles.

11.2 CPU Features

- Single cycle instruction execution (20 ns cycle time @ 50 MHz, 13.3 ns @ 75 MHz)
- DC to 50 MHz operation (75 MHz on selected chips)
- User selectable clock options: (Internal R/C, External R/C, resonator, crystal oscillator or crystal-oscillator pack)
- Internal R/C oscillator (31 KHz to 4 MHz, +/- 8% accuracy)
- 43 single-word basic instructions
- 2048 x 12-bits (4096 x 12-bits in SX48/52) E^2Flash program memory rated for 10,000 rewrite cycles
- Up to 137 bytes (262 bytes in SX48/52) of directly, or indirectly, addressable RAM
- Selectable 8-level hardware stack
- Fixed interrupt response time: 60 ns internal, 100 ns external
- Hardware context save/restore of PC, W, STATUS, and FSR on interrupt.
- Multi-Input Wake-Up (MIWU) on 8 pins
- In-system programming via OSC pins
- Single-step and breakpoint debugging via OSC2 pin
- Analog comparator (RB0 out, RB1 in-, RB2 in+)
- Built-in brown-out detector (On/Off, 4.2V) (4.2, 2.6, 2.2, Off in SX48/52)
- W mappable into RTCC space for flexibility
- Nine sources of interrupts (17 in SX48/52)
- 1998 UL compliance and fast lookup provided through run-time readable code

11.3 Peripheral and I/O Features

- Every pin programmable as input or output
- Inputs are each TTL or CMOS level selectable
- All pins include selectable internal pull-ups (~20 kΩ to V_{DD})
- RB, RC, RD and RE inputs each selectable as Schmitt Trigger

11 Appendix A: SX Features

- All outputs capable of sinking/sourcing 30 mA
- Symmetrical drive on RA outputs (same Vdrop +/-)
- Two 16-bit timers count clock cycles, external events and generate interrupts and external signals (SX48/52 only)

12 Appendix B: Instruction Set Overview

12.1 Introduction

The instruction set of the SX20/28/48/52 microcontrollers consists of 43 single-word basic instructions that are executed in one clock cycle, with the exception of JMP, CALL, and failed test instructions, like DECSZ, INCSZ, SB and SNB.

In addition to the 43 basic instructions, the SX-Key assembler allows for additional instruction mnemonics that are either converted internally into other basic instructions, or are expanded into two or more basic instructions.

12.2 Instruction Set Summary

Table 22 – SX Instruction Mnemonics below, contains a list of all instruction mnemonics supported by the assembler:

12 Appendix B: Instruction Set Overview

Table 22 - SX Instruction Mnemonics

Instruction	Parameters	Meaning
ADD	dest, src	ADD
ADDB	dest, {/} src_bit	ADD bit to destination register
AND	dest, src	AND
BANK	dest	Switch to RAM Bank indicated by dest
CALL	addr8	CALL
CJA	op1, op2, addr9	Compare, Jump if Above
CJAE	op1, op2, addr9	Compare, Jump if Above or Equal
CJB	op1, op2, addr9	Compare, Jump if Below
CJBE	op1, op2, addr9	Compare, Jump if Below or Equal
CJNE	op1, op2, addr9	Compare, Jump if not Equal
CLC		CLear Carry flag
CLR	dest	CLeaR
CLRB	dest_bit	CLeaR Bit
CLZ		CLear Zero flag
CSA	op1, op2	Compare, Skip if Above
CSAE	op1, op2	Compare, Skip if Above or Equal
CSB	op1, op2	Compare, Skip if Below
CSBE	op1, op2	Compare, Skip of Below or Equal
CSE	op1, op2	Compare, Skip if Equal
CSNE	op1, op2	Compare, Skip if Not Equal
DEC	dest	DECrement
DECSZ	dest	DECrement, Skip if Zero
DJNZ	dest, addr9	Decrement, Jump if Not Zero
IJNZ	dest, addr9	Increment, Jump if Not Zero
INC	dest	INCrement
INCSZ	dest	INCrement, Skip if Zero
IREAD		Indirect READ
JB	op_bit, addr9	Jump if Bit
JC	addr9	Jump if Carry
JMP	addr9	JuMP
JNB	op_bit, addr9	Jump if Not Bit
JNC	addr9	Jump if Not Carry
JNZ	addr9	Jump if Not Zero
JZ	addr9	Jump if Zero
MODE	lit	MODE
MOV	{!}dest, {!, / ,-- , ++, <<, >>, <>} src {-dest}	MOVe
MOVB	dest_bit, {/}src_bit	MOVe Bit
MOVSZ	dest, [++ | --]src	MOVe, Skip if Zero
NOP		NO Operation
NOT	dest	NOT

12 Appendix B: Instruction Set Overview

Instruction	Parameters	Meaning
OR	dest, src	OR
PAGE	addr12	PAGE
RET		RETurn from subroutine
RETI		RETurn from Interrupt
RETIW		RETurn from Interrupt with RTCC = RTCC+W
RETP		RETurn from subroutine with Page restore
RETW	lit{, lit…}	RETurn from subroutine with W set to lit
RL	dest	Rotate Left
RR	dest	Rotate Right
SB	src_bit	Skip if Bit
SC		Skip if Carry
SETB	dest_bit	SET Bit
SKIP		SKIP
SLEEP		SLEEP
SNB	src_bit	Skip if Not Bit
SNC		Skip if Not Carry
SNZ		Skip if Not Zero
STC		SeT Carry
STZ		SeT Zero
SUB	dest, src	SUBtract
SUBB	dest, {/}src_bit	SUBtract bit from destination reg.
SWAP	dest	SWAP nibbles
SZ		Skip if Zero
TEST	dest	TEST for zero
XOR	dest, src	eXclusive OR

{} = optional [|] = choice one of to or more
addr8 = 8-bit address addr9 = 9-bit address
addr12 = 11-bit address (SX20/28) or 12-bit address (SX48/52)
dest = destination dest_bit = destination bit
lit = literal op1/op2 = first/second operand
src = source src_bit = source bit

12.3 Single Word Instructions

Table 23 - SX Single-Word Instructions on the next two pages lists all instructions that consume just one word of the SX E²Flash program memory:

Table 23 - SX Single-Word Instructions

Instr.	Parameters	Meaning
ADD	fr, W	fr + W ⇨ fr
ADD	W, fr	fr + W ⇨ W
AND	fr, W	fr AND W ⇨ fr
AND	W, fr	fr AND W ⇨ W
AND	W, #literal	W AND literal ⇨ W
BANK	fr	fr(7:5)⇨ FSR(7:5) (SX20/28) / fr(7:5)⇨ FSR(6:4) (SX48/52)
CALL	addr8	PC ⇨ TOS, addr8 ⇨ PC(7:0)
CLC		0 ⇨ C
CLR	fr	0 ⇨ fr
CLR	W	0 ⇨ W
CLR	!WDT	0 ⇨ !WDT
CLRB	op.bit	0 ⇨ op.bit
CLZ		0 ⇨ Z
DEC	fr	fr-1 ⇨ fr
DECSZ	fr	fr-1 ⇨ fr, PC+1 ⇨ PC when fr = 0
INC	fr	fr+1 ⇨ fr
INCSZ	fr	fr+1 ⇨ fr, PC+1 ⇨ PC when fr = 0
IREAD		(M:W) ⇨ M:W
JMP	addr9	addr9(8:0) ⇨ PC(8:0), STATUS(7:5) ⇨ PC(11:9)
JMP	W	W ⇨ PC(7:0)
JMP	PC+W	PC(7:0)+W ⇨ PC(7:0)
MODE	literal	literal(3:0) ⇨ M(3:0)
MOV	fr, W	W ⇨ fr
MOV	W, fr	fr ⇨ W
MOV	W, /fr	NOT fr ⇨ W
MOV	W, fr-W	fr-W ⇨ W
MOV	W, ++fr	fr+1 ⇨ W
MOV	W, --fr	fr-1 ⇨ W
MOV	W, <<fr	RL fr ⇨ W
MOV	W, >>fr	RR fr ⇨ W
MOV	W, <>fr	fr(7:4) ⇨ W(3:0), fr(3:0) ⇨ W(7:4)
MOV	W, #literal	literal ⇨ W
MOV	W, M	M ⇨ W
MOV	M, #literal	literal ⇨ M
MOV	M, W	W ⇨ M
MOV	!OPTION, W	W ⇨ !OPTION
MOV	!port, W	W ⇨ !port
MOVSZ	W, ++fr	fr+1 ⇨ W, PC+1 ⇨ PC when W = 0
MOVSZ	W, --fr	fr-1 ⇨ W, PC+1 ⇨ PC when W = 0

Instr.	Parameters	Meaning
NOP		
NOT	fr	NOT fr ⇨ fr
NOT	W	NOT W ⇨ W
OR	fr, W	fr OR W ⇨ fr
OR	W, fr	fr OR W ⇨ W
OR	W, #literal	W OR literal ⇨ W
PAGE	addr12	addr12(10:9) ⇨ STATUS(6:5) (SX20/28) / addr12(11:9) ⇨ STATUS(7:5) (SX48/52)
RET		TOS ⇨ PC
RETI		Restores W, STATUS, FSR and PC from shadow registers
RETIW		RTCC+W ⇨ RTCC, restores W, STATUS, FSR and PC from shadow registers
RETP		TOS(10:9) ⇨ PA1:PA0, TOS(8:0) ⇨ PC
RETW	lit	lit ⇨ W, TOS ⇨ PC
RL	fr	C ⇨ fr(0), fr(6:0) ⇨ fr(7:1), fr(7) ⇨ C
RR	fr	C ⇨ fr(7), fr(7:1) ⇨ fr(6:0), fr(0) ⇨ C
SB	op.bit	PC+1 ⇨ PC, when bit is set in op
SC		PC+1 ⇨ PC, when C is set
SETB	op.bit	1 ⇨ bit in op
SKIP		PC+1 ⇨ PC
SLEEP		
SNB	op.bit	PC+1 ⇨ PC when bit is clear in op
SNC		PC+1 ⇨ PC when C is clear
SNZ		PC+1 ⇨ PC when Z is clear
STC		1 ⇨ C
STZ		1 ⇨ Z
SUB	fr, W	fr-W ⇨ fr
SWAP	fr	fr(7:4) ⇨ fr(3:0), fr(3:0) ⇨ fr(7:4)
SZ		PC+1 ⇨ PC when Z is set
TEST	fr	NOT(fr-fr) ⇨ Z
TEST	W	NOT(W-W) ⇨ Z
XOR	fr, W	fr XOR W ⇨ fr
XOR	W, fr	fr XOR W ⇨ fr
XOR	W, #literal	W XOR literal ⇨ W

addr8 = 8-bit address addr9 = 9-bit address
addr12 = 11-bit (SX20/28) or 12-bit (SX48/52) address
bit = bit position (0…7) in operand C = carry flag
fr = file register (location in RAM) FSR = file select register
M = mode register op = operand
!OPTION = option register PC = program counter register
!port = port configuration register RTCC = real-time clock counter register
STATUS = status register TOS = top of stack
W = working register !WDT = watchdog timer register
Z = zero flag

12.4 Multi-Word Instructions

The instructions in **Table 24 - SX Multi-Word Instructions** are translated into two or more single word instructions by the assembler.

Important: *All single-word skip instructions (see* ***Table 23 - SX Single-Word Instructions****) advance the program counter by one only. Therefore, make sure that a skip is* ***never*** *immediately followed by a multi-word instruction, because this will most likely generate a lot of trouble. Also note that most of the multi-word instructions make use of W as a temporary register, without preserving its original value.*

Table 24 - SX Multi-Word Instructions

Instr.	Parameters	Translates to			
ADD	fr, #lit	MOV W, #lit	MOV fr, W		
ADD	fr1, fr2	MOV W, fr2	ADD fr1, W		
ADDB	fr, op.bit	SNB op.bit	INC fr		
ADDB	fr, /op.bit	SB op.bit	INC fr		
AND	fr, #lit	MOV W, #lit	AND fr, W		
AND	fr1, fr2	MOV W, fr2	AND fr1, W		
CJA	fr, #lit, addr9	MOV W, #lit ^ $FF	ADD W, fr	SNC	JMP addr9
CJA	fr1, fr2, addr9	MOV W, fr1	MOV W, fr2-W	SC	JMP addr9
CJAE	fr, #lit, addr9	MOV W, #lit	MOV W, fr-W	SNC	JMP addr9
CJAE	fr1, fr2, addr9	MOV W, fr2	MOV W, fr1-W	SNC	JMP addr9
CJB	fr, #lit, addr9	MOV W, #lit	MOV W, fr-W	SC	JMP addr9
CJB	fr1, fr2, addr9	MOV W, fr2	MOV W, fr1-W	SC	JMP addr9
CJBE	fr, #lit, addr9	MOV W, #lit ^ $FF	ADD W, fr	SC	JMP addr9
CJBE	fr1, fr2, addr9	MOV W, fr1	MOV W, fr2-W	SNC	JMP addr9
CJE	fr, #lit, addr9	MOV W, #lit	MOV W, fr-W	SNZ	JMP addr9
CJE	fr1, fr2, addr9	MOV W, fr2	MOV W, fr1-W	SNZ	JMP addr9
CJNE	fr, #lit, addr9	MOV W, #lit	MOV W, fr-W	SZ	JMP addr9
CJNE	fr1, fr2, addr9	MOV W, fr2	MOV W, fr1-W	SZ	JMP addr9
CSA	fr, #lit	MOV W, #lit ^ $FF	ADD W, fr	SC	
CSA	fr1, fr2	MOV W, fr1	MOV W, fr2 – W	SNC	
CSAE	fr, #lit	MOV W, #lit	MOV W, fr-W	SC	
CSAE	fr1, fr2	MOV W, fr2	MOV W, fr1-W	SC	
CSB	fr, #lit	MOV W, #lit	MOV W, fr-W	SNC	
CSB	fr1, fr2	MOV W, fr2	MOV W, fr1-W	SNC	
CSBE	fr, #lit	MOV W, #lit ^ $FF	ADD W, fr	SNC	
CSBE	fr1, fr2	MOV W, fr1	MOV W, fr2-W	SC	
CSE	fr, #lit	MOV W, #lit	MOV W, fr-W	SZ	
CSE	fr1, fr2	MOV W, fr2	MOV W, fr1-W	SZ	
CSNE	fr, #lit	MOV W, #lit	MOV W, fr-W	SNZ	
CSNE	fr1, fr2	MOV W, fr2	MOV W, fr1-W	SNZ	
DJNZ	fr, addr9	DECSZ fr	JMP addr9		
IJNZ	fr, addr9	INCSZ fr	JMP addr9		
JB	op.bit, addr9	SNB op.bit	JMP addr9		
JC	addr9	SNC	JMP addr9		

12 Appendix B: Instruction Set Overview

Instr.	Parameters	Translates to			
JNB	op.bit, addr9	SB op.bit	JMP addr9		
JNC	addr9	SC	JMP addr9		
JNZ	addr9	SZ	JMP addr9		
JZ	addr9	SNZ	JMP addr9		
MOV	fr, #lit	MOV W, #lit	MOV fr, W		
MOV	fr1, fr2	MOV W, fr2	MOV fr1, W		
MOV	fr, M	MOV W, M	MOV fr, W		
MOV	M, fr	MOV W, fr	MOV M, W		
MOV	!OPTION, fr	MOV W, fr	MOV !OPTION, W		
MOV	!OPTION, #lit	MOV W, #lit	MOV !OPTION, W		
MOV	!port, fr	MOV W, fr	MOV !port, W		
MOV	!port, #lit	MOV W, #lit	MOV !port, W		
MOVB	op1.bit1, op2.bit2	SB op2.bit2	CLRB op1.bit1	SNB op2.bit2	SETB op1.bit1
MOVB	op1.bit1, /op2.bit2	SNB op2.bit2	CLRB op1.bit1	SB op2.bit2	SETB op1.bit1
OR	fr, #lit	MOV W, #lit	OR fr, W		
OR	fr1, fr2	MOV W, fr2	OR fr1, W		
RETW	lit1{, lit2, …}	RETW #lit	{RETW #lit}…		
SUB	fr, #lit	MOV W, #lit	SUB fr, W		
SUB	fr1, fr2	MOV W, fr2	SUB fr1, W		
SUBB	fr, op.bit	SNB op.bit	DEC fr		
SUBB	fr, /op.bit	SB op.bit	DEC fr		
XOR	fr, #lit	MOV W, #lit	XOR fr, W		
XOR	fr1, fr2	MOV W, fr2	XOR fr1, W		

addr8 = 8-bit address addr9 = 9-bit address
addr12 = 12-bit address bit = bit position (0…7) in operand
C = carry flag fr = file register (location in RAM)
FSR = file select register M = mode register
op = operand !OPTION = option register
PC = program counter register !port = port configuration register
RTCC = real-time clock counter register STATUS = status register
TOS = top of stack W = working register
!WDT = watchdog timer register Z = zero flag

12.5 Instruction Set Quick Reference

This chart is a quick reference to command syntax, size, cycle time, CARRYX sensitivity and affected flags and registers. An explanation of the abbreviations used, can be found on the next page.

Table 25 - SX Instruction Set Quick Reference

Instruction		Affects	W	C
ADD	fr,W	fr C DC Z	1	1
ADD	fr1,[#lit | fr2]	fr1 W C DC Z	2	2
ADD	W,fr	W C DC Z	1	1
ADDB	fr,{/}op.bit	fr Z	2	2
AND	fr,W	fr Z	1	1
AND	fr1,[#lit | fr2]	fr1 W Z	2	2
AND	W,[#lit | fr]	W Z	1	1
BANK	fr	FSR	1	1
CALL	addr8	PC	1	3
CJA	fr1,[#lit | fr2],addr9	W C DC Z	4	4,6
CJAE	fr1,[#lit | fr2],addr9	W C DC Z	4	4,6
CJB	fr1,[#lit | fr2],addr9	W C DC Z	4	4,6
CJBE	fr1,[#lit | fr2],addr9	W C DC Z	4	4,6
CJE	fr1,[#lit | fr2],addr9	W C DC Z	4	4,6
CJNE	fr1,[#lit | fr2],addr9	W C DC Z	4	4,6
CLC		C	1	1
CLR	[fr | W | !WDT]	[fr Z | W Z | (*1)]	1	1
CLRB	op.bit	op.bit	1	1
CLZ		Z	1	1
CSA	fr1,[#lit | fr2]	W C DC Z	3	3,4
CSAE	fr1,[#lit | fr2]	W C DC Z	3	3,4
CSB	fr1,[#lit | fr2]	W C DC Z	3	3,4
CSBE	fr1,[#lit | fr2]	W C DC Z	3	3,4
CSE	fr1,[#lit | fr2]	W C DC Z	3	3,4
CSNE	fr1,[#lit | fr2]	W C DC Z	3	3,4
DEC	fr	fr Z	1	1
DECSZ	fr	fr	1	1,2
DJNZ	fr,addr9	fr Z PC	2	2,4
IJNZ	fr,addr9	fr Z PC	2	2,4
INC	fr	fr Z	1	1
INCSZ	fr	fr	1	1,2
IREAD		MODE W	1	4
JB	op.bit,addr9	PC	2	2,4
JC	addr9	PC	2	2,4
JMP	[addr9 | W]	PC	1	3
JMP	[W | PC+W]	[PC | PC C DC Z]	1	3
JNB	op.bit,addr9	PC	2	2,4
JNC	addr9	PC	2	2,4
JNZ	addr9	PC	2	2,4
JZ	addr9	PC	2	2,4
MODE	lit	M	1	1
MOV	fr, W	fr	1	1
MOV	fr1,[#lit | fr2]	[fr1 W | fr1 W Z]	2	2
MOV	fr,M	fr W	2	2
MOV	W,{/ | ++ | --}fr	W Z	1	1
MOV	W,{<< | >>}fr	W C	1	1
MOV	W,<>fr	W	1	1
MOV	W,fr-W	W C DC Z	1	1
MOV	W,[#lit | M]	W	1	1
MOV	M,fr	W M Z	2	2
MOV	M,[#lit | W]	M	1	1
MOV	!OPTION,[fr | #lit]	[W Z OPT | W OPT]	2	2
MOV	!OPTION,W	OPT	1	1
MOV	!port,[fr | #lit]	[W Z !port | W !port]	2	2
MOV	!port,W	!port (W)	1	1
MOVB	op1.bit1,{/}op2.bit2	op1.bit1	4	4
MOVSZ	W, [++ | --]	W	1	1,2
NOP		none	1	1
NOT	[fr | W]	[fr Z | W Z]	1	1
OR	fr,W	fr Z	1	1
OR	fr1,[#lit | fr2]	fr1 W Z	2	2
OR	W,[fr, #lit]	W Z	1	1
PAGE	addr12	PAx	1	1
RET		PC	1	3
RETI		C DC Z PAx PC W	1	3
RETIW		RTCC (*2)	1	3
RETP		PAx, PC	1	3
RETW	#lit{,#lit...}	PC W	x	3*x
RL	fr	fr C	1	1
RR	fr	fr C	1	1
SB	op.bit	PC	1	1,2
SC		PC	1	1,2
SETB	op.bit	op.bit	1	1
SKIP		PC	1	2
SLEEP		WDT TO PD	1	1
SNB	op.bit	PC	1	1,2
SNC		PC	1	1,2
SNZ		PC	1	1,2
STC		C	1	1,2
STZ		Z	1	1,2
SUB	fr1,[#lit | fr2]	fr1 W C DC Z	2	2
SUB	fr,W	fr C DC Z	1	1
SUBB	fr,{/}op.bit	fr Z	2	2
SWAP	fr	fr	1	1
SZ		PC	1	1,2
TEST	[fr | W]	Z	1	1
XOR	fr1,[#lit | fr2]	fr1 W Z	2	2
XOR	fr,W	fr Z	1	1
XOR	W,[fr | #lit]	W Z	1	1

12 Appendix B: Instruction Set Overview

{}	= optional
[|]	= choice one of many
#,#	= no branch / branch cycles in column "C"
C	= cycles in Turbo mode (with a few exceptions, in non-Turbo mode, instructions take 4 times longer)
grayed	= adversely affected when CARRYX is specified
W	= number of words that are used for the instruction
x	= one word per RETW parameter
(*1)	= TO and PD flags are affected
(*2)	= in addition to the flags/registers affected by RETI

The "Affects" column lists the registers and flags that may be affected by the instruction. When two or more choices "[|]" for an instruction are specified that affect different registers of flags, the "Affects" column similarly lists the alternatives in square brackets, separated by a " | " character.

For example, JMP [W | PC+w] [PC | PC C DC Z] means that JMP W affects PC and JMP PC+w affects PC, C, DC, and Z.

13 Appendix C: SX Instruction Set

13.1 Introduction

The columns of each instruction definition table in this appendix contain important information about the instruction's behavior, size and structure.

The Command column lists all the available forms of the given command. The operands in lower-case letters indicate a symbol or value should be inserted in their place. The operands in upper-case letters should be entered exactly as seen. For example, the following form of the MOV command:

```
MOV !OPTION, #literal
```

should be entered into code (assuming $A5 is the desired literal) as follows:

```
MOV !OPTION, #$A5
```

The operands are described in **Table 26 - Symbol and Value Operands,** below.

Table 26 - Symbol and Value Operands

Symbol	Definition
addr8	An 8-bit address symbol or value
addr9	A 9-bit address symbol or value
addr12	An 11-bit (SX20/28) or 12-bit (SX48/52) address symbol or value
fr	A file register
#literal	A literal value ('#' must precede value)
M	The mode register
op.bit	The specified bit of the specified operand
!OPTION	The option register
PC	The program counter
!port	The specified I/O port data direction reg.
W	The working register
!WDT	The watchdog register

The *Words* column indicates the number of 12-bit EEPROM words consumed by the instruction.

The *Cycles* column indicates the number of clock cycles the given instruction will take. The number outside of parenthesis is the number of cycles in Turbo mode. The number inside parenthesis is the number of cycles in non-Turbo mode (compatibility mode).

13 Appendix C: SX Instruction Set

The *Affects* column indicates the flags and registers the given instruction may affect. Depending on the kind of instruction, flags and/or registers are always affected, or only on certain results of the instruction. **Table 27 - Flags and Registers**, below, describes these flags and registers.

Table 27 - Flags and Registers

Symbol	Definition
C	The carry flag
DC	The digit-carry flag
FSR	The file select register
fr	The file register
M	The mode register
op.bit	The specified bit of the specified operand
OPT	The options register
PC	The program counter
PD	The power-down flag
!port	The specified I/O port data direction register
TO	The time-out flag
W	The working register
Z	The zero flag

The Coding column indicates how the given command will assemble, including binary values and mnemonic instructions. Some commands assemble into multiple, simpler commands. **Table 28 - Binary Symbols,** below, describes the binary symbols.

Table 28 - Binary Symbols

Symbol	Definition
b	Bit address
f	File register address
k	Constant

Any instruction that performs a skip will only skip one instruction word. To avoid strange results, care must be taken to make sure that a single word instruction immediately follows the skipping instruction.

An exception to this rule are skip instructions that are immediately followed by a BANK or PAGE instruction. Here (provided that the tested condition is true), two instructions will be skipped, i.e. the BANK or PAGE instruction plus the next one. This is useful for conditional branching to another page where a PAGE instruction precedes a JMP. If several PAGE and BANK instructions immediately follow a skip instruction then they are all skipped plus the next instruction and a clock cycle is consumed for each.

Many instructions are adversely affected by the carry flag when CARRYX (Add/Sub with C) is specified. Be careful to follow the special notes within the instruction descriptions concerning this.

ADD dest, src — Add src into dest

Command	Words	Cycles	Affects	Coding
1) ADD fr, W	1	1 (4)	fr, C, DC, Z	0001 111f ffff ADD fr, W
2) ADD fr, #literal	2	2 (8)	fr, W, C, DC, Z	1100 kkkk kkkk MOV W, #lit 0001 111f ffff ADD fr, W
3) ADD fr1, fr2	2	2 (8)	fr, W, C, DC, Z	0010 000f ffff MOV W, fr2 0001 111f ffff ADD fr1, W
4) ADD W, fr	1	1 (8)	W, C, DC, Z	0001 110f ffff ADD W, fr

Operation: src is added into dest. C will be set if an overflow occurs; otherwise, C will be cleared. DC will be set if an overflow occurs in the lower nibble; otherwise, DC will be cleared. Z will be set if the result is 0; otherwise, Z will be cleared. W is left holding the source value in command #2 and #3. *If CARRYX is specified, C is added to result. Insert a CLC before the first Add on a register to avoid strange results.*

ADDB dest, src_bit — Add src_bit into dest

Command	Words	Cycles	Affects	Coding
1) ADDB fr, op.bit	2	2 (8)	fr, Z	0110 bbbf ffff SNB op.bit 0010 101f ffff INC fr
2) ADDB fr, /op.bit	2	2 (8)	fr, Z	0111 bbbf ffff SB op.bit 0010 101f ffff INC fr

Operation: src_bit is added into dest. If fr is incremented, Z will be set if the result is 0; otherwise, Z will be cleared. This instruction is useful for adding the carry into the upper byte of a double-byte sum after the lower byte has been computed.

AND dest, src — AND src into dest

Command	Words	Cycles	Affects	Coding
1) AND fr, W	1	1 (4)	fr, Z	0001 011f ffff AND fr, W
2) AND fr, #literal	2	2 (8)	fr, W, Z	1100 kkkk kkkk MOV W, #lit 0001 011f ffff AND fr, W
3) AND fr1, fr2	2	2 (8)	fr1, W, Z	0010 000f ffff MOV W, fr2 0001 011f ffff AND fr1, W
4) AND W, fr	1	1 (4)	W, Z	0001 010f ffff AND W, fr
5) AND W, #literal	1	1 (4)	W, Z	1110 kkkk kkkk AND W, #lit

Operation: src is ANDed into dest. Z will be set if the result is 0; otherwise, Z will be cleared. W is left holding the source value in command #2 and #3.

BANK dest — Set bank select bits

Command	Words	Cycles	Affects	Coding
BANK fr	1	1 (4)	FSR	0000 0001 1fff BANK fr

Operation: Writes file registers bits 7 through 5 (on the SX20/28) or 6 through 4 (on the SX48/52) to the same bits in the file select register (FSR) in preparation for a RAM access across a bank boundary. The full 8-bit file register address must be used as the destination. *On the SX48/52, bit 7 in the FSR is used to select between upper and lower block of banks. This bit is not affected by the BANK instruction, and must be set or cleared with a separate SETB FSR.7 or CLRB FSR.7 following the BANK instruction.*

CALL addr8 — Call subroutine with 8-bit address

Command	Words	Cycles	Affects	Coding
1) CALL addr8	1	3 (8)	PC	1001 kkkk kkkk CALL addr8

Operation: The next instruction address is pushed onto the stack and addr8 is moved to the program counter. The ninth bit of the program counter will be cleared to 0. Therefore, calls are only allowed to the first half of any 512-word page, although the CALL instruction can be anywhere.

CJA op1, op2, addr9 — Compare op1 to op2 and jump if above

Command	Words	Cycles	Affects	Coding
1) CJA fr, #literal, addr	4	4 or 6 (jump) (16 or 20)	W, C, DC, Z	1100 kkkk kkkk MOV W, #lit^$FF 0001 110f ffff ADD W, fr 0110 0000 0011 SNC 101k kkkk kkkk JMP addr9
2) CJA fr1, fr2, addr	4	4 or 6 (jump) (16 or 20)	W, C, DC, Z	0010 000f ffff MOV W, fr1 0000 100f ffff MOV W, fr2-W 0111 0000 0011 SC 101k kkkk kkkk JMP addr9

Operation: op1 is compared to op2. If op1 is greater than op2, a jump to addr9 is executed. W is left holding the result of op1 + ~op2 in command #1 and op2 - op1 in command #2. *If CARRYX is specified, c affects the result. Insert a CLC before command #1 and an STC before command #2 to avoid strange results.*

CJAE op1, op2, addr9 — Compare op1 to op2 and jump if above or equal

Command	Words	Cycles	Affects	Coding

1) CJAE fr, #literal, addr9	4	4 or 6 (jump)
		(16 or 20)
			W, C, DC, Z	`1100 kkkk kkkk MOV W, #lit`
				`0000 100f ffff MOV W, fr-W`
				`0110 0000 0011 SNC`
				`101k kkkk kkkk JMP addr9`

2) CJAE fr1, fr2, addr9	4	4 or 6 (jump)
		(16 or 20)
			W, C, DC, Z	`0010 000f ffff MOV W, fr2`
				`0000 100f ffff MOV W, fr1-W`
				`0110 0000 0011 SNC`
				`101k kkkk kkkk JMP addr9`

Operation: op1 is compared to op2. If op1 is greater than or equal to op2, a jump to addr9 is executed. W is left holding the result of op2 - op1. *If CARRYX is specified, c affects the result. Insert an STC before command to avoid strange results.*

CJB op1, op2, addr9 — Compare op1 to op2 and jump if below

Command	Words	Cycles	Affects	Coding

1) CJB fr, #literal, addr9	4	4 or 6 (jump)
		(16 or 20)
			W, C, DC, Z	`1100 kkkk kkkk MOV W, #lit`
				`0000 100f ffff MOV W, fr-W`
				`0111 0000 0011 SC`
				`101k kkkk kkkk JMP addr9`

2) CJB fr1, fr2, addr9	4	4 or 6 (jump)
		(16 or 20)
			W, C, DC, Z	`0010 000f ffff MOV W, fr2`
				`0000 100f ffff MOV W, fr1-W`
				`0111 0000 0011 SC`
				`101k kkkk kkkk JMP addr9`

Operation: op1 is compared to op2. If op1 is less than op2, a jump to addr9 is executed. W is left holding the result of op2 - op1. *If CARRYX is specified, c affects the result. Insert an STC before command to avoid strange results.*

CJBE op1, op2, addr9 — Compare op1 to op2 and jump if below or equal

Command	Words	Cycles	Affects	Coding

1) CJBE fr, #literal, addr9	4	4 or 6 (jump)
		(16 or 20)
			W, C, DC, Z	`1100 kkkk kkkk MOV W, #lit^$FF`
				`0001 110f ffff ADD W, fr`
				`0111 0000 0011 SC`
				`101k kkkk kkkk JMP addr9`

2) CJBE fr1, fr2, addr9	4	4 or 6 (jump)
		(16 or 20)
			W, C, DC, Z	`0011 000f ffff MOV W, fr1`
				`0000 100f ffff MOV W, fr2-W`
				`0110 0000 0011 SNC`
				`101k kkkk kkkk JMP addr9`

Operation: op1 is compared to op2. If op1 is less than or equal to op2, a jump to addr9 is executed. W is left holding the result of ~op2 + op1 in command #1 and op2 - op1 in command #2. *If CARRYX is specified, c affects the result. Insert a CLC before command #1 and an STC before command #2 to avoid strange results.*

CJE op1, op2, addr9 — Compare op1 to op2 and jump if equal

Command	Words	Cycles	Affects	Coding

1) CJE fr, #literal, addr9	4	4 or 6 (jump) (16 or 20)	W, C, DC, Z	`1100 kkkk kkkk MOV W, #lit`
				`0000 100f ffff MOV W, fr-W`
				`0110 0100 0011 SNZ`
				`101k kkkk kkkk JMP addr9`

2) CJE fr1, fr2, addr9	4	4 or 6 (jump) (16 or 20)	W, C, DC, Z	`0010 000f ffff MOV W, fr2`
				`0000 100f ffff MOV W, fr1-W`
				`0110 0100 0011 SNZ`
				`101k kkkk kkkk JMP addr9`

Operation: op1 is compared to op2. If op1 is equal to op2, a jump to addr9 is executed. W is left holding the result of op1 - op2. *If CARRYX is specified, c affects the result. Insert an STC before command to avoid strange results.*

CJNE op1, op2, addr9 — Compare op1 to op2 and jump if not equal

Command	Words	Cycles	Affects	Coding

1) CJNE fr, #literal, addr9	4	4 or 6 (jump) (16 or 20)	W, C, DC, Z	`1100 kkkk kkkk MOV W, #lit`
				`0000 100f ffff MOV W, fr-W`
				`0111 0100 0011 SZ`
				`101k kkkk kkkk JMP addr9`

2) CJNE fr1, fr2, addr9	4	4 or 6 (jump) (16 or 20)	W, C, DC, Z	`0010 000f ffff MOV W, fr2`
				`0000 100f ffff MOV W, fr1-W`
				`0111 0100 0011 SZ`
				`101k kkkk kkkk JMP addr9`

Operation: op1 is compared to op2. If op1 is not equal to op2, a jump to addr9 is executed. W is left holding the result of op1 - op2. *If CARRYX is specified, c affects the result. Insert an STC before command to avoid strange results.*

CLC — Clear carry

Command	Words	Cycles	Affects	Coding
1) CLC	1	1 (4)	C	`0100 0000 0011 CLC`

Operation: The C flag is cleared to 0.

CLR dest — Clear dest

Command	Words	Cycles	Affects	Coding
1) CLR fr	1	1 (4)	fr, Z	0000 011f ffff CLR fr
2) CLR W	1	1 (4)	W, Z	0000 0100 0000 CLR w
3) CLR !WDT	1	1 (4)	TO, PD	0000 0000 0100 CLR wdt

Operation: dest is cleared to 0. Z is set to 1 in command #1 and #2 while TO and PD are set to 1 in command #3. Prescaler is also cleared in command #3, if assigned.

CLRB dest_bit — Clear dest_bit

Command	Words	Cycles	Affects	Coding
1) CLRB op.bit	1	1 (4)	op.bit	0100 bbbf ffff CLRB op.bit

Operation: dest_bit is cleared to 0.

CLZ — Clear zero

Command	Words	Cycles	Affects	Coding
1) CLZ	1	1 (4)	Z	0100 0100 0011 CLZ

Operation: The Z flag is cleared to 0.

CSA op1, op2 — Compare op1 to op2 and skip if above

Command	Words	Cycles	Affects	Coding
1) CSA fr, #literal	3	3 or 4 (skip) (12 or 16)	W, C, DC, Z	1100 kkkk kkkk MOV W, #lit^$FF 0001 110f ffff ADD W, fr 0111 0000 0011 SC
2) CSA fr1, fr2	3	3 or 4 (skip) (12 or 16)	W, C, DC, Z	0010 000f ffff MOV W, fr1 0000 100f ffff MOV W, fr2-W 0110 0000 0011 SNC

Operation: op1 is compared to op2. If op1 is greater than op2, the following instruction word is skipped. W is left holding the result of op1 + ~op2 in command #1 and op2 - op1 in command #2. *If CARRYX is specified, c affects the result. Insert a CLC before command #1 and an STC before command #2 to avoid strange results.*

Note: Only one word is skipped by this instruction. *To avoid strange results, make sure that any instruction following CSA is a single-word instruction.*

CSAE op1, op2 — Compare op1 to op2 and skip if above or equal

Command	Words	Cycles	Affects	Coding

1) CSAE fr, #literal	3	3 or 4 (skip)
		(12 or 16)
			W, C, DC, Z	`1100 kkkk kkkk MOV W, #lit`
				`0000 100f ffff MOV W, fr-W`
				`0111 0000 0011 SC`

2) CSAE fr1, fr2	3	3 or 4 (skip)
		(12 or 16)
			W, C, DC, Z	`0010 000f ffff MOV W, fr2`
				`0000 100f ffff MOV W, fr1-W`
				`0111 0000 0011 SC`

Operation: op1 is compared to op2. If op1 is greater than or equal to op2, the following instruction word is skipped. W is left holding the result of op1 - op2. *If CARRYX is specified, c affects the result. Insert an STC before command to avoid strange results.*

Note: Only one word is skipped by this instruction. *To avoid strange results, make sure that any instruction following CSAE is a single-word instruction.*

CSB op1, op2 — Compare op1 to op2 and skip if below

Command	Words	Cycles	Affects	Coding

1) CSB fr, #literal	3	3 or 4 (skip)
		(12 or 16)
			W, C, DC, Z	`1100 kkkk kkkk MOV W, #lit`
				`0000 100f ffff MOV W, fr-W`
				`0110 0000 0011 SNC`

2) CSB fr1, fr2	3	3 or 4 (skip)
		(12 or 16)
			W, C, DC, Z	`0010 000f ffff MOV W, fr2`
				`0000 100f ffff MOV W, fr1-W`
				`0110 0000 0011 SNC`

Operation: op1 is compared to op2. If op1 is less than op2, the following instruction word is skipped. W is left holding the result of op1 - op2. *If CARRYX is specified, c affects the result. Insert an STC before command to avoid strange results.*

Note: Only one word is skipped by this instruction. *To avoid strange results, make sure that any instruction following CSB is a single-word instruction.*

CSBE op1, op2 — Compare op1 to op2 and skip if below or equal

Command	Words	Cycles	Affects	Coding

1) CSBE fr, #literal	3	3 or 4 (skip) (12 or 16)	W, C, DC, Z	`1100 kkkk kkkk MOV W, #lit^$FF`
				`0001 110f ffff ADD W, fr`
				`0110 0000 0011 SNC`

2) CSBE fr1, fr2	3	3 or 4 (skip) (12 or 16)	W, C, DC, Z	`0010 000f ffff MOV W, fr1`
				`0000 100f ffff MOV W, fr2-W`
				`0111 0000 0011 SC`

Operation: op1 is compared to op2. If op1 is less than or equal to op2, the following instruction word is skipped. W is left holding the result of op1 + ~op2 in command #1 and op2 - op1 in command #2. *If CARRYX is specified, c affects the result. Insert a CLC before command #1 and an STC before command #2 to avoid strange results.*

Note: Only one word is skipped by this instruction. *To avoid strange results, make sure that any instruction following CSBE is a single-word instruction.*

CSE op1, op2 — Compare op1 to op2 and skip if equal

Command	Words	Cycles	Affects	Coding

1) CSE fr, #literal	3	3 or 4 (skip) (12 or 16)	W, C, DC, Z	`1100 kkkk kkkk MOV W, #lit`
				`0000 100f ffff MOV W, fr-W`
				`0111 0100 0011 SZ`

2) CSE fr1, fr2	3	3 or 4 (skip) (12 or 16)	W, C, DC, Z	`0010 000f ffff MOV W, fr2`
				`0000 100f ffff MOV W, fr1-W`
				`0111 0100 0011 SZ`

Operation: op1 is compared to op2. If op1 is equal to op2, the following instruction word is skipped. W is left holding the result of op1 - op2. *If CARRYX is specified, c affects the result. Insert an STC before command to avoid strange results.*

Note: Only one word is skipped by this instruction. *To avoid strange results, make sure that any instruction following CSE is a single-word instruction.*

CSNE op1, op2 — Compare op1 to op2 and skip if not equal

Command	Words	Cycles	Affects	Coding

1) CSNE fr, #literal	3	3 or 4 (skip)
		(12 or 16)
			W, C, DC, Z	`1100 kkkk kkkk MOV W, #lit`
				`0000 100f ffff MOV W, fr-W`
				`0110 0100 0011 SNZ`

2) CSNE fr1, fr2	3	3 or 4 (skip)
		(12 or 16)
			W, C, DC, Z	`0010 000f ffff MOV W, fr2`
				`0000 100f ffff MOV W, fr1-W`
				`0110 0100 0011 SNZ`

Operation: op1 is compared to op2. If op1 is not equal to op2, the following instruction word is skipped. W is left holding the result of op1 - op2. *If CARRYX is specified, c affects the result. Insert an STC before command to avoid strange results.*

Note: Only one word is skipped by this instruction. *To avoid strange results, make sure that any instruction following CSNE is a single-word instruction.*

DEC dest — Decrement dest

Command	Words	Cycles	Affects	Coding
1) DEC fr	1	1 (4)	fr, Z	`0000 111f ffff DEC fr`

Operation: dest is decremented. Z will be set to 1 if the result was 0; otherwise, Z will be cleared to 0. *The MOV W, --fr command is similar to DEC fr, except the result is moved to W, and fr keeps its original contents.*

DECSZ dest — Decrement dest and skip if zero

Command	Words	Cycles	Affects	Coding
1) DECSZ fr	1	1 or 2 (skip) (4 or 8)	fr	`0010 111f ffff DECSZ fr`

Operation: dest is decremented. If result is 0, the next instruction word will be skipped.

Note: Only one word is skipped by this instruction. *To avoid strange results, make sure that any instruction following DECSZ is a single-word instruction.*

DJNZ dest, addr9 — Decrement dest and jump if not zero

Command	Words	Cycles	Affects	Coding
1) DJNZ fr, addr9	2	2 or 4 (jump) (8 or 12)	fr, Z, PC	`0010 111f ffff DECSZ fr` `101k kkkk kkkk JMP addr9`

Operation: dest is decremented. If the result is not 0, a jump to addr9 is executed. Z will be set to 1 if the result was 0; otherwise, Z will be cleared to 0.

IJNZ dest, addr9 — Increment dest and jump if not zero

Command	Words	Cycles	Affects	Coding
1) IJNZ fr, addr9	2	2 or 4 (jump) (8 or 12)	fr, Z, PC	`0011 111f ffff INCSZ fr` `101k kkkk kkkk JMP addr9`

Operation: dest is incremented. If the result is not 0, a jump to addr9 is executed. Z will be set to 1 if the result was 0; otherwise, Z will be cleared to 0.

INC dest — Increment dest

Command	Words	Cycles	Affects	Coding
1) INC fr	1	1 (4)	fr, Z	`0010 101f ffff INC fr`

Operation: dest is incremented. Z will be set to 1 if the result was 0; otherwise, Z will be cleared to 0. *The MOV W,++fr command is similar to INC fr, except the result is moved to W, and fr keeps its original contents.*

INCSZ dest — Increment dest and skip if zero

Command	Words	Cycles	Affects	Coding
1) INCSZ fr	1	1 or 2 (skip) (4 or 8)	fr	`0011 111f ffff INCSZ fr`

Operation: dest is incremented. If the result is 0, the next instruction word will be skipped.

Note: *Only one word is skipped by this instruction. To avoid strange results, make sure that any instruction following INCSZ is a single-word instruction.*

13 Appendix C: SX Instruction Set

IREAD — Read instruction at MODE:W into MODE:W

Command	Words	Cycles	Affects	Coding
1) IREAD	1	4 (16)	MODE, W	`0000 0100 0001 IREAD`

Operation: The instruction or value at the 12-bit location MODE:W is read and stored into the MODE:W bits. This instruction can be used to read values in tables created with the DW directive. Use the MODE and MOV instructions to read and write from the mode register.

JB src_bit, addr9 — Jump if src_bit is set

Command	Words	Cycles	Affects	Coding
1) JB op.bit, addr9	2	2 or 4 (jump) (8 or 12)	PC	`0110 bbbf ffff SNB op.bit` `101k kkkk kkkk JMP addr9`

Operation: If src_bit is set, a jump to addr9 is executed.

JC addr9 — Jump if carry

Command	Words	Cycles	Affects	Coding
1) JC addr9	2	2 or 4 (jump) (8 or 12)	PC	`0110 0000 0011 SNC` `101k kkkk kkkk JMP addr9`

Operation: If the carry flag is set, a jump to addr9 is executed.

JMP dest — Jump to dest

Command	Words	Cycles	Affects	Coding
1) JMP addr9	1	3 (8)	PC	`101k kkkk kkkk JMP addr9`
2) JMP W	1	3 (8)	PC	`0000 001f ffff JMP w`
3) JMP PC+W	1	3 (8)	PC, C, DC, Z	`0001 111f ffff ADD PC, W`

Operation: Jump to address in dest. The lower 9 bits of the literal addr9 are moved into the program counter in command #1. W is moved into the program counter in command #2. W+1 is added to the program counter in command #3. Bit 9 of the program counter is cleared in command #2 and #3, so the jump destination will be in the first 256 words of any 512-word page. This instruction is useful for jumping into lookup tables comprised of RETW instructions, or jumping to particular routines. The flags are set as in an ADD instruction for command #3. *If CARRYX is specified, c affects the result of command #3. Insert a CLC before command #3 to avoid strange results.*

JNB src_bit, addr9 — Jump if src_bit is not set

Command	Words	Cycles	Affects	Coding
1) JNB op.bit, addr9	2	2 or 4 (jump) (8 or 12)	PC	`0111 bbbf ffff SB op.bit` `101k kkkk kkkk JMP addr9`

Operation: If src_bit is not set, a jump to addr9 is executed.

JNC addr9 — Jump if carry is not set

Command	Words	Cycles	Affects	Coding
1) JNC addr9	2	2 or 4 (jump) (8 or 12)	PC	`0111 0000 0011 SC` `101k kkkk kkkk JMP addr9`

Operation: If the carry flag is not set, a jump to addr9 is executed.

JNZ addr9 — Jump if zero in not set

Command	Words	Cycles	Affects	Coding
1) JNZ addr9	2	2 or 4 (jump) (8 or 12)	PC	`0111 0100 0011 SZ` `101k kkkk kkkk JMP addr9`

Operation: If the zero flag is not set, a jump to addr9 is executed.

JZ addr9 — Jump if zero is set

Command	Words	Cycles	Affects	Coding
1) JZ addr9	2	2 or 4 (jump) (8 or 12)	PC	`0110 0100 0011 SNZ` `101k kkkk kkkk JMP addr9`

Operation: If the zero flag is set, a jump to addr9 is executed.

MODE src — Set Mode to src

Command	Words	Cycles	Affects	Coding
1) MODE literal	1	1 (4)	M	`0000 0101 kkkk MOV M, #lit`

Operation: The lower 4 bits of src are moved into the Mode register. This command is the same as MOV M, #literal. Use this command to initiate mode changes for port configuration commands. *Since the SX48/52 requires a 5-bit Mode register, use MOV W, #lit followed by MOV M, W to affect all 5 bits.*

MOV dest, src — Move src into dest

Command	Words	Cycles	Affects	Coding
1) MOV fr, W	1	1 (4)	fr	`0000 001f ffff MOV fr, W`
2) MOV fr, #literal	2	2 (8)	fr, W	`1100 kkkk kkkk MOV W, #lit` `0000 001f ffff MOV fr, W`
3) MOV fr1, fr2	2	2 (8)	fr1, W, Z	`0010 000f ffff MOV W, fr2` `0000 001f ffff MOV fr1, W`
4) MOV fr, M	2	2 (8)	fr, W	`0000 0100 0010 MOV W, M` `0000 001f ffff MOV fr, W`
5) MOV W, fr	1	1 (4)	W, Z	`0010 000f ffff MOV W, fr`
6) MOV W, /fr	1	1 (4)	W, Z	`0010 010f ffff MOV W, /fr`
7) MOV W, fr-W	1	1 (4)	W, C, DC, Z	`0000 100f ffff MOV fr-W`
8) MOV W, ++fr	1	1 (4)	W, Z	`0010 100f ffff MOV W, ++fr`
9) MOV W, --fr	1	1 (4)	W, Z	`0000 110f ffff MOV W, --fr`
10) MOV W, <<fr	1	1 (4)	W, C	`0011 010f ffff MOV W, <<fr`
11) MOV W, >>fr	1	1 (4)	W, C	`0011 000f ffff MOV W, >>fr`
12) MOV W, <>fr	1	1 (4)	W	`0011 100f ffff MOV W, <>fr`
13) MOV W, #literal	1	1 (4)	W	`1100 kkkk kkkk MOV W, #lit`
14) MOV W, M	1	1 (4)	W	`0000 0100 0010 MOV W, M`
15) MOV M, fr	2	2 (8)	W, M, Z	`0010 000f ffff MOV W, fr` `0000 0100 0011 MOV M, W`
16) MOV M, W	1	1 (4)	M	`0000 0100 0011 MOV M, W`
17) MOV M, #literal	1	1 (4)	M	`0000 0101 kkkk MOV M, #lit`
18) MOV !OPTION, fr	2	2 (8)	W, Z, OPT	`0010 000f ffff MOV W, fr` `0000 0000 0010 MOV !OPT, W`
19) MOV !OPTION, W	1	1 (4)	OPT	`0000 0000 0010 MOV !OPT, W`
20) MOV !OPTION, #literal	2	2 (8)	W, OPT	`1100 kkkk kkkk MOV W, #lit` `0000 0000 0010 MOV !OPT, W`
21) MOV !port, fr	2	2 (8)	W, Z, !port	`0010 000f ffff MOV W, fr` `0000 0000 0fff MOV !port, W`
22) MOV !port, W	1	1 (4)	!port, (W)	`0000 0000 0fff MOV !port, W`
23) MOV !port, #literal	2	2 (8)	W, !port	`1100 kkkk kkkk MOV W, #lit` `0000 0000 0fff MOV !port, W`

Operation: Src is moved into dest. Z will be set if the result is 0; otherwise, Z will be cleared. W is left holding the source value in command number 2, 3, 4, 18, 20, 21 and 23. C will be cleared if an underflow occurred; otherwise, C will be set to 1 in command number 7, 10 and 11. DC will be cleared if an underflow occurred in the lowest nibble; otherwise, DC will be set in command number 7. The value of C will be shifted into the LSB or MSB of W in command #10 and #11, respectively. C will be set to the previous MSB or LSB of fr in command #10 and #11 respectively. Command #12 moves the nibble-swapped value of fr into w. Instructions #6 through #12 are similar to NOT, SUB, INC, DEC, RL, RR and SWAP instructions, respectively, but have the additional feature of moving the result to W. *Only 4 bits are affected by #17; use #13 followed by #16 to affect 5 bits in the SX48/52. If CARRYX is specified, c affects the result of command #7. Insert an STC before command #7 to avoid strange results.*

MOVB dest_bit, src_bit — Move src_bit to dest_bit

Command	Words	Cycles	Affects	Coding

1) MOVB op.bit1, op.bit2	4	4 (16)	op.bit1	`0111 bbbf ffff SB op.bit2`
				`0100 bbbf ffff CLRB op.bit1`
				`0110 bbbf ffff SNB op.bit2`
				`0101 bbbf ffff SETB op.bit1`

2) MOVB op.bit1, /op.bit2	4	4 (16)	op.bit1	`0110 bbbf ffff SNB op.bit2`
				`0100 bbbf ffff CLRB op.bit1`
				`0111 bbbf ffff SB op.bit2`
				`0101 bbbf ffff SETB op.bit1`

Operation: src_bit is moved into dest_bit in command #1. The one's complement of src_bit is moved into dest_bit in command #2.

MOVSZ dest, src — Move incremented or decremented src to dest and skip if zero

Command	Words	Cycles	Affects	Coding
1) MOVSZ W, ++fr	1	1 or 2 (skip) (4 or 8)	W	`0011 110f ffff MOVSZ W, ++fr`
2) MOVSZ W, --fr	1	1 or 2 (skip) (4 or 8)	W	`0010 110f ffff MOVSZ W, --fr`

Operation: The incremented value (command #1) or decremented value (command #2) of src is moved into dest. The next instruction word will be skipped if the result was 0.

Note: Only one word is skipped by this instruction. *To avoid strange results, make sure that any instruction following MOVSZ is a single-word instruction.*

NOP — No operation

Command	Words	Cycles	Affects	Coding
1) NOP	1	1 (4)	none	`0000 0000 0000 NOP`

Operation: None. This instruction is useful to adjust the timing of a routine.

NOT dest — Not dest

Command	Words	Cycles	Affects	Coding
1) NOT fr	1	1 (4)	fr, Z	`0010 011f ffff NOT fr`
2) NOT W	1	1 (4)	W, Z	`1111 1111 1111 NOT w`

Operation: dest is converted into its one's complement value. Z will be set if the result was 0; otherwise, Z will be cleared. *The MOV W,/fr command is similar to #1, except the result is moved to W, and fr keeps its original contents.*

OR dest, src — OR src into dest

Command	Words	Cycles	Affects	Coding
1) OR fr, W	1	1 (4)	fr, Z	`0001 001f ffff OR fr, W`
2) OR fr, #literal	2	2 (8)	fr, W, Z	`1100 kkkk kkkk MOV W, #lit` `0001 001f ffff OR fr, W`
3) OR fr1, fr2	2	2 (8)	fr, W, Z	`0010 000f ffff MOV W, fr2` `0001 001f ffff OR fr, W`
4) OR W, fr	1	1 (4)	W, Z	`0001 000f ffff OR W, fr`
5) OR W, #literal	1	1 (4)	W, Z	`1101 kkkk kkkk OR W, #lit`

Operation: src is OR'd into dest. Z will be set if the result was 0; otherwise, Z will be cleared.

PAGE addr12 — Set page select bits

Command	Words	Cycles	Affects	Coding
1) PAGE addr12	1	1 (4)	PAx	`0000 0001 0fff PAGE addr`

Operation: Writes upper address bits into status register in preparation for a jump or call across a page boundary. On the SX20/28, address bits 10 and 9 are written into status register bits 6 and 5. On the SX48/52, address bits 11 through 9 are written into status register bits 7 through 5. Status register bits 7 though 5 are also called PA2 through PA0.

RET — Return from subroutine

Command	Words	Cycles	Affects	Coding
1) RET	1	3 (8)	PC	`0000 0000 1100 RET`

Operation: The top stack value is moved into the program counter and execution proceeds with the instruction following the most recent call instruction.

RETI — Return from interrupt routine

Command	Words	Cycles	Affects	Coding
1) RETI	1	3 (8)	C, DC, Z, PAx, PC, W, FSR	`0000 0000 1110 RETI`

Operation: W, STATUS (except TO & PD), FSR and PC are popped off the shadow registers and execution proceeds with the instruction following the jump to interrupt.

RETIW — Return from interrupt routine, adjust RTCC

Command	Words	Cycles	Affects	Coding
1) RETIW	1	3 (8)	C, DC, Z, PAx, PC, W, FSR, RTCC	`0000 0000 1111 RETIW`

Operation: The value in W is added to RTCC, then W, STATUS (except TO & PD), FSR and PC are popped off the shadow registers and execution proceeds with the instruction following the jump to interrupt. This is useful to create jitter-free, timed interrupts when using the interrupt-on-timer-rollover feature.

RETP — Return from subroutine across a page boundary

Command	Words	Cycles	Affects	Coding
1) RETP	1	3 (8)	PAx, PC	`0000 0000 1101 RETP`

Operation: The top stack value is moved into the program counter, upper return address bits are written to the page select bits (bit 10:9 to status register 6:5 on SX20/28, or bits 11:9 to status register bits 7:5 on SX48/52), and execution proceeds with the instruction following the most recent call instruction. This instruction allows returning from a subroutine across page boundaries.

RETW value — Assemble RETWs which load W with literal data upon return

Command	Words	Cycles	Affects	Coding
1) RETW #literal {, #literal...}	1 per literal	3 (8) per literal	PC, W	`1000 kkkk kkkk RETW #lit` `{1000 kkkk kkkk RETW #lit...}`

Operation: A list of RETWs is assembled each with one literal. This list can be accessed by JMP PC+W or JMP W instructions. This is useful for lookup tables.

RL dest — Rotate dest left

Command	Words	Cycles	Affects	Coding
1) RL fr	1	1 (4)	fr, C	`0011 011f ffff RL fr`

Operation: dest is rotated left one bit. On entry, C must hold the value to be shifted into the least-significant bit of the dest value. On exit, C will hold the previous most-significant bit of the dest value. *The MOV W,<<fr command is similar to RL fr, except the result is moved to W, and fr keeps its original contents.*

RR dest — Rotate dest right

Command	Words	Cycles	Affects	Coding
1) RR fr	1	1 (4)	fr, C	`0011 001f ffff RR fr`

Operation: dest is rotated right one bit. On entry, C must hold the value to be shifted into the most-significant bit of the dest value. On exit, C will hold the previous least-significant bit of the dest value. *The MOV W,>>fr command is similar to RR fr, except the result is moved to W, and fr keeps its original contents.*

SB src_bit — Skip if src_bit is set

Command	Words	Cycles	Affects	Coding
1) SB op.bit	1	1 or 2 (skip) (4 or 8)	PC	`0111 bbbf ffff SB op.bit`

Operation: If src_bit is set, the following instruction word is skipped.

Note: Only one word is skipped by this instruction. *To avoid strange results, make sure that any instruction following SB is a single-word instruction.*

SC — Skip if carry is set

Command	Words	Cycles	Affects	Coding
1) SC	1	1 or 2 (skip) (4 or 8)	PC	`0111 0000 0011 SC`

Operation: If C is set, the following instruction word is skipped.

Note: Only one word is skipped by this instruction. *To avoid strange results, make sure that any instruction following SC is a single-word instruction.*

SETB src_bit — Set src_bit

Command	Words	Cycles	Affects	Coding
1) SETB op.bit	1	1 (4)	op.bit	`0101 bbbf ffff SETB op.bit`

Operation: src_bit is set to 1.

SKIP — Skip the following instruction word

Command	Words	Cycles	Affects	Coding
1) SKIP	1	2 (8)	PC	`0110 0000 0010 SKIP`

Operation: The following instruction word is skipped.

Note: Only one word is skipped by this instruction. *To avoid strange results, make sure that any instruction following SKIP is a single-word instruction.*

SLEEP — Enter sleep mode

Command	Words	Cycles	Affects	Coding
1) SLEEP	1	1 (4)	WDT, TO, PD	`0000 0000 0011 SLEEP`

Operation: The watchdog timer is cleared and the oscillator is stopped. TO is set and PD is cleared.

SNB src_bit — Skip if src_bit not set

Command	Words	Cycles	Affects	Coding
1) SNB op.bit	1	1 or 2 (skip) (4 or 8)	PC	`0110 bbbf ffff SNB op.bit`

Operation: If src_bit is cleared, the following instruction word is skipped.

Note: Only one word is skipped by this instruction. *To avoid strange results, make sure that any instruction following SNB is a single-word instruction.*

SNC — Skip if carry not set

Command	Words	Cycles	Affects	Coding
1) SNC	1	1 or 2 (skip) (4 or 8)	PC	`0110 0000 0011 SNC`

Operation: If C is cleared, the following instruction word is skipped.

Note: Only one word is skipped by this instruction. *To avoid strange results, make sure that any instruction following SNC is a single-word instruction.*

SNZ — Skip if zero is not set

Command	Words	Cycles	Affects	Coding
1) SNZ	1	1 or 2 (skip) (4 or 8)	PC	`0110 0100 0011 SNZ`

Operation: If Z is cleared, the following instruction word is skipped.

Note: Only one word is skipped by this instruction. *To avoid strange results, make sure that any instruction following SNZ is a single-word instruction.*

STC — Set carry flag

Command	Words	Cycles	Affects	Coding
1) STC	1	1 (4)	C	`0101 0000 0011 STC`

Operation: The C flag is set.

STZ — Set zero flag

Command	Words	Cycles	Affects	Coding
1) STZ	1	1 (4)	Z	`0101 0100 0011 STZ`

Operation: The Z flag is set.

SUB dest, src — Subtract src from dest

Command	Words	Cycles	Affects	Coding
1) SUB fr, W	1	1 (4)	fr, C, DC, Z	0000 101f ffff SUB fr, W
2) SUB fr1, #literal	2	2 (8)	fr, W, C, DC, Z	1100 kkkk kkkk MOV W, #lit 0000 101f ffff SUB fr, W
3) SUB fr1, fr2	2	2 (8)	fr, W, C, DC, Z	0010 000f ffff MOV W, fr 0000 101f ffff SUB fr, W

Operation: src is subtracted from dest. C will be cleared to 0 if an underflow occurred; otherwise, C will be set to 1. DC will be cleared to 0 if an underflow occurred in the least-significant nibble. Z will be set to 1 if the result was 0; otherwise, Z will be cleared to 0. The MOV W, fr-W command is similar to #1, except the result is moved to W, and fr keeps its original contents. *If CARRYX is specified, c is added to the result. Insert an STC before the first Sub on a register to avoid strange results.*

SUBB dest, src_bit — Subtract src_bit from dest

Command	Words	Cycles	Affects	Coding
1) SUBB fr, op.bit	2	2 (8)	fr, Z	0110 bbbf ffff SNB op.bit 0000 111f ffff DEC fr
1) SUBB fr, /op.bit	2	2 (8)	fr, Z	0111 bbbf ffff SB op.bit 0000 111f ffff DEC fr

Operation: Subtracts src_bit from dest. If dest was decremented, Z will be set if the result was zero; else, Z will be cleared. This instruction is useful for subtracting the carry from the upper byte of a double-byte value after the lower byte has been subtracted.

SWAP dest — Swap nibbles in dest

Command	Words	Cycles	Affects	Coding
1) SWAP fr	1	1 (4)	fr	0011 101f ffff SWAP fr

Operation: The high- and low-order nibbles of dest are swapped. The MOV W,<>fr command is similar to SWAP fr, except the result is moved to W, and fr keeps its original contents.

SZ — Skip if zero flag set

Command	Words	Cycles	Affects	Coding
1) SZ	1	1 or 2 (skip) (4 or 8)	PC	`0111 0100 0011 SZ`

Operation: If Z is set, the following instruction word is skipped.

Note: Only one word is skipped by this instruction. *To avoid strange results, make sure that any instruction following SZ is a single-word instruction.*

TEST src — Test src for zero

Command	Words	Cycles	Affects	Coding
1) TEST fr	1	1 (4)	Z	`0010 001f ffff TEST fr`
2) TEST w	1	1 (4)	Z	`1101 0000 0000 TEST w`

Operation: The Z flag will be set if src is 0; otherwise, Z will be cleared.

XOR dest, src — XOR src into dest

Command	Words	Cycles	Affects	Coding
1) XOR fr, W	1	1 (4)	fr, Z	`0001 101f ffff XOR fr, W`
2) XOR fr, #literal	2	2 (8)	fr, W, Z	`1100 kkkk kkkk MOV W, #lit` `0001 101f ffff XOR fr, W`
3) XOR fr1, fr2	2	2 (8)	fr, W, Z	`0010 000f ffff MOV W, fr2` `0001 101f ffff XOR fr1, W`
4) XOR W, fr	1	1 (4)	W, Z	`0001 100f ffff XOR W, fr`
5) XOR W, #literal	1	1 (4)	W, Z	`1111 kkkk kkkk XOR W, #lit`

Operation: src is XOR'd into dest. Z will be set if the result was zero; otherwise, Z will be cleared.

14 Appendix D: The SX Tech Board

The Parallax SX Tech Board is a learning tool for 28-pin DIP SX microcontrollers. The led28.src file, included with the SX-Key installation program, demonstrates a simple program using the SX Tech Board and the SX28 microcontroller.

Figure 17 - The SX Tech Board

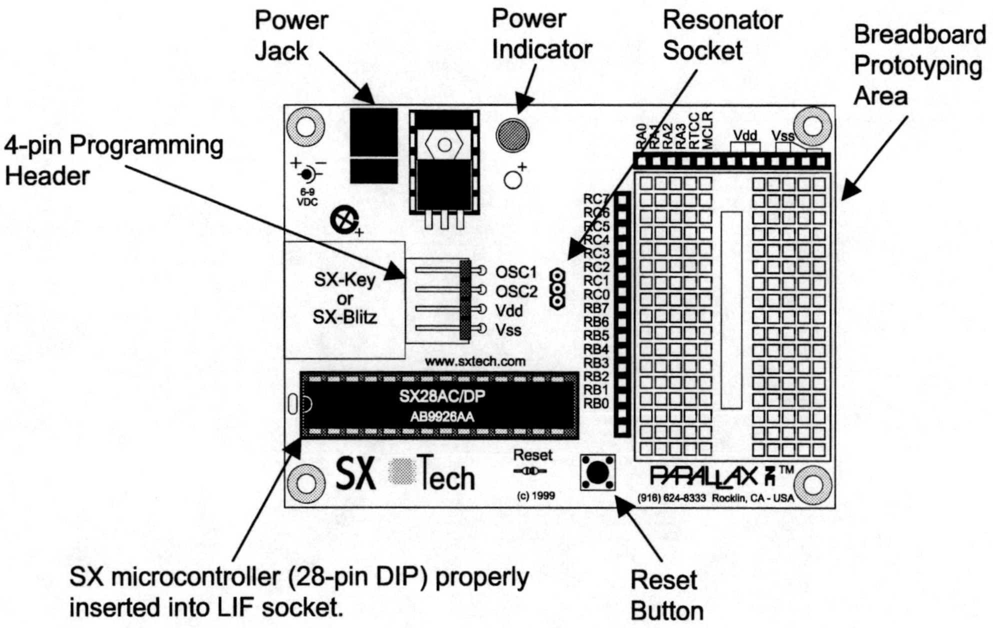

14.1 SX Tech Board Features

The SX Tech Board contains a socket and breadboard area to make development with the 28-pin SX DIP microcontroller easier. *The SX Tech Board only supports the SX-28 chip.*

The SX Tech Board contains the following items:

- 7.5 VDC, 1A center positive power supply input
- Power indicator (LED)
- 28-pin LIF socket
- 50 MHz ceramic resonator (in 3-pin socket)

14 Appendix D: The SX Tech Board

- Breadboard area for prototyping
- I/O pin headers adjacent to breadboard
- Reset button

14.2 Connecting and Downloading

See **Chapter 3.1 – Connecting and Downloading to the SX Tech Board** for steps to connect and use the SX-Tech Board with the led28.src program.

14.3 SX Tech Board Schematic

Figure 18 - SX Tech Board Schematic

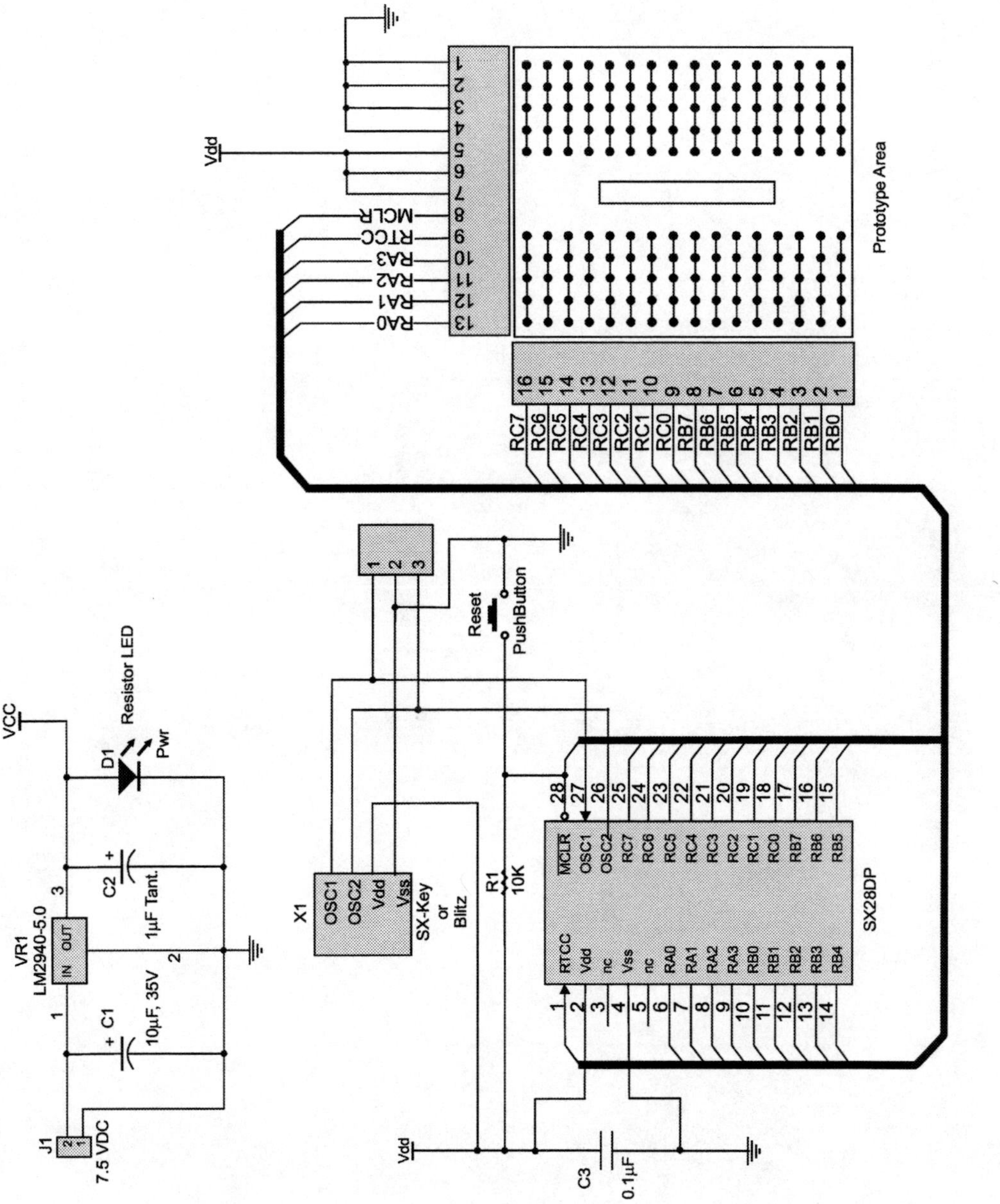

15 Appendix E: SX Data Sheet

15.1 Pinout Information and Descriptions

Figure 19 - SX Pinouts

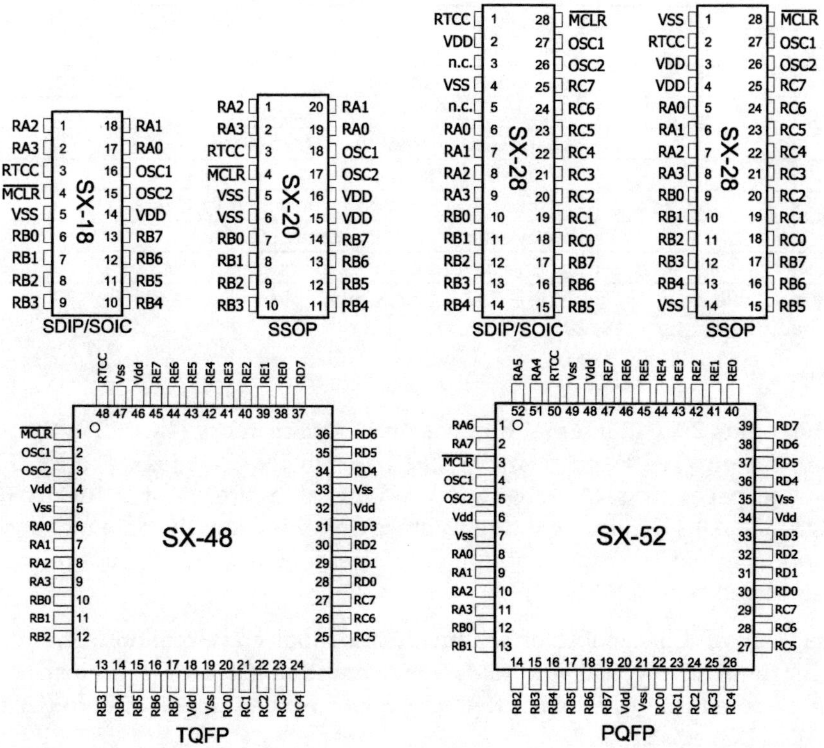

Note: Drawings are not to scale or proportion. Some devices are no longer available from Ubicom, they are shown here for completeness only.

15 Appendix E: SX Data Sheet

Table 29 - SX Pins

Name	Type	Input Levels	Description
RA0 – RA7*	I/O	TTL/CMOS	Bi-directional I/O Pin, Complimentary Drive
RB0 - RB2	I/O	TTL/CMOS/ST	Bi-directional I/O Pin; MIWU mode; Comparator output, - input, + input
RB3 - RB7	I/O	TTL/CMOS/ST	Bi-directional I/O Pin; MIWU mode; (SX48/52 RB4 – RB7: T1 capture input 1, 2, PWM/compare out, ext. clock source)
RC0 - RC7*	I/O	TTL/CMOS/ST	Bi-directional I/O Pin (SX48/52 RC0 – RC3: T2 capture input 1, 2, PWM/compare out, external clock source)
RD0 – RE7*	I/O	TTL/CMOS/ST	Bi-directional I/O Pin
RTCC	I	ST	Input to Real Time Clock/Counter
$\overline{\text{MCLR}}$	I	ST	Master Clear (reset) input (active low).
OSC1	I	ST	Oscillator crystal input - external clock input.
OSC2	I/O	CMOS	Weakly pulled to Vdd internally on RC mode.
Vdd	P	-	Positive supply for logic and I/O pins.
Vss	P	-	Ground Reference for logic and I/O pins.

* RA4 – RA7 is only available on the SX52, RD0 – RE7 are only available on the SX48/52, RC0 – RC7 is not available on the SX18/20

15.2 Architecture

The Ubicom SX chip offers 2K x 12 internal EE/Flash program memory (4K x 12 in the SX48/52) and up to 137 bytes of general purpose RAM memory (262 bytes in the SX48/52). The EE/Flash memory is organized in 512-word pages. The RAM memory is addressable directly or indirectly (as well as semi-directly in the SX48/52). All special function registers are mapped into the data memory. Configuration registers do not appear in data memory and are only accessible through the use of the MODE register and the port configuration commands.

The ALU is 8-bits wide and is capable of arithmetic and Boolean operations. The 'W' register is the working register for the ALU. Typically, it holds one operand in a two-operand instruction. Depending on the instruction executed, the ALU may affect the values of the Carry (C), Zero (Z), and Digit Carry (DC) flags of the STATUS register.

The SX chip comes equipped with special features that reduce system cost and power requirements. The Power-On Reset (POR) and Device Reset Timer eliminate the need for external reset circuitry. The power saving SLEEP mode, watchdog timer, and code protect features reduce system cost and improve system integrity.

15.2.1 Instruction Pipeline

Figure 20 - Instruction Pipeline

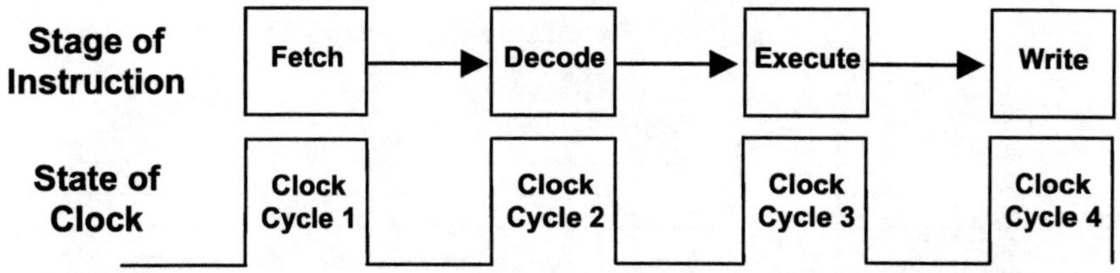

There are several stages an instruction must go through to actually execute within the SX chip. Specifically, there are four stages that are collectively referred to as the pipeline, and are shown in **Figure 20 - Instruction Pipeline**. The first instruction is fetched from memory on the first clock cycle. On the second clock cycle the first instruction is decoded and the second instruction is fetched. On the third clock cycle the first instruction is executed, the second instruction is decoded, and the third instruction is fetched. On the fourth clock cycle the first instruction's results are written to its destination, the second instruction is executed, the third instruction is decoded and the fourth instruction is fetched. Once the pipeline is full, instructions are executed at the rate of one per clock cycle (in Turbo mode). Instructions that directly alter the value in the program counter, i.e. jumps, calls, etc. require that the pipeline be cleared and subsequently refilled. When the pipeline is cleared, the fetch and decode stages are replaced with 'nop' instructions. This effectively nullifies the invalid instructions and increases the cycle-time for that command by 3 cycles.

15.2.2 Read-Modify-Write Considerations

Use caution when performing successive SETB or CLRB operations on an I/O port pin. Since input data used for an instruction must be valid *during* the time the instruction is executed, and the result output from an instruction is valid *after* that instruction completes its operation, unexpected results from successive read-modify-write operations on I/O pins can occur when the SX is running at extremely high speeds. The SX has an internal write-back section to prevent such data errors from occurring but it is recommended that you buffer successive read-modify-write instructions performed on I/O pins of the same port at extremely high clock rates with a 'nop' instruction.

Also note, a read of an I/O pin actually reads the pin, not the output data latch. That is, if an output driver on a pin is enabled and driven high, but the external circuit is holding it low, a read of the port pin will indicate that the pin is low. Of course, externally driving an I/O pin while the output latch is driving it will result in damage to the SX chip. Care should be taken to not do this.

15.2.3 Register Map Structure

The SX20/28 RAM memory consists of a global bank of special function registers and eight banks of 16 general-purpose registers. The SX48/52 RAM memory consists of a global bank of special function registers and 16 banks of 16 general-purpose registers. **Figure 21 – SX20/28 Register Map** and **Figure 22**

– **SX48/52 Register Map** demonstrate the structure of the registers for the SX20/28 and the SX48/52, respectively. In all SX instructions, bit 4 of the register address operand determines whether the global registers are accessed or whether a bank of general-purpose registers is accessed.

Figure 21 - SX20/28 Register Map

SX20/28 Register Map

	Global		Bank 0	Bank 1	Bank 2		Bank 7
$00-	IND	$10-	$0	$0	$0		$0
$01-	RTCC	$11-	$1	$1	$1		$1
$02-	PC	$12-	$2	$2	$2		$2
$03-	Status	$13-	$3	$3	$3		$3
$04-	FSR	$14-	$4	$4	$4		$4
$05-	Port A	$15-	$5	$5	$5		$5
$06-	Port B	$16-	$6	$6	$6		$6
$07-	Port C*	$17-	$7	$7	$7	•••	$7
$08-	$08	$18-	$8	$8	$8		$8
$09-	$09	$19-	$9	$9	$9		$9
$0A-	$0A	$1A-	$A	$A	$A		$A
$0B-	$0B	$1B-	$B	$B	$B		$B
$0C-	$0C	$1C-	$C	$C	$C		$C
$0D-	$0D	$1D-	$D	$D	$D		$D
$0E-	$0E	$1E-	$E	$E	$E		$E
$0F-	$0F	$1F-	$F	$F	$F		$F

*Port C is available as general-purpose RAM in the SX20.

Figure 22 - SX48/52 Register Map

SX48/52 Register Map

	Global		Bank 0*	Bank 1	Bank 2		Bank 15
$00-	IND	$10-	$0	$0	$0		$0
$01-	RTCC	$11-	$1	$1	$1		$1
$02-	PC	$12-	$2	$2	$2		$2
$03-	Status	$13-	$3	$3	$3		$3
$04-	FSR	$14-	$4	$4	$4		$4
$05-	Port A	$15-	$5	$5	$5		$5
$06-	Port B	$16-	$6	$6	$6		$6
$07-	Port C	$17-	$7	$7	$7	•••	$7
$08-	Port D	$18-	$8	$8	$8		$8
$09-	Port E	$19-	$9	$9	$9		$9
$0A-	$0A	$1A-	$A	$A	$A		$A
$0B-	$0B	$1B-	$B	$B	$B		$B
$0C-	$0C	$1C-	$C	$C	$C		$C
$0D-	$0D	$1D-	$D	$D	$D		$D
$0E-	$0E	$1E-	$E	$E	$E		$E
$0F-	$0F	$1F-	$F	$F	$F		$F

* Bank 0 is available only when using semi-direct addressing.

15.2.4 Special Function Registers

Special function registers are registers used by the CPU to control the operation of the device. The special function registers are contained within the first seven to ten locations of the global RAM bank as shown above and are described below.

Table 30 - Special Function Registers

Addr.	Name	Function
$00	IND	Used for indirect addressing
$01	RTCC/WREG	Real Time Clock Counter/WREG
$02	PC	Program Counter (low byte)
$03	STATUS	Holds status bits of ALU
$04	FSR	File Select Register
$05	RA	Port A register
$06	RB	Port B register
$07	RC	Port C register *
$08	RD	Port D register *
$09	RE	Port E register *

* RC, RD and RE are available as general purpose RAM in the SX20. RD and RE are available as general purpose RAM in the SX28.

15.2.5 IND – The Indirect Register ($00)

This register, though not physically implemented, is used for indirect addressing. An instruction using IND as its operand actually performs the operation on the register pointed to by the contents of FSR. See Indirect Addressing, below, for more information.

15.2.6 Real Time Clock/Counter, WREG ($01)

RTCC is an 8-bit real-time timer/counter. In timer mode, the RTCC register will increment with every instruction cycle (without prescaler). In counter mode, the RTCC will increment with every cycle on the RTCC pin (with prescaler). The prescaler is used to lengthen the RTCC or watchdog timer effectively up to 16-bits. Depending on the RTW bit (OPTION.7), register $01 contains either the RTCC, (RTW is set) or the WREG, (RTW cleared). When WREG exists at $01, file register instructions (INC, DECSZ, etc) can be used directly on WREG. When doing this, use the register address $01, or the WREG symbol, rather than W. Using the W symbol instead of WREG to operate directly on the working register will result in errors or incorrectly assembled code.

15.2.7 PC – Program Counter ($02)

PC is a register that holds the lower 8-bits of the program counter. It is accessible at runtime to perform computed jumps and determine return addresses. Whenever an instruction is executed, and PC is the destination, the upper 2 or 3 bits of the STATUS register are loaded into the high byte of the program counter (bit 8 of the program counter is either cleared (CALL), or taken from the instruction opcode

(JMP). This is necessary to achieve computed jumps and subroutine calls *across* page boundaries in code memory. Only 11 bits are used in SX20/28 parts. See The Jump Instruction for examples detailing how the program counter and the STATUS register are used in typical situations.

15.2.8 STATUS Register ($03)

This register holds the arithmetic status of the ALU, the page select bits, and the reset status. The status register is accessible during run-time but the reset bits, PD and TO, are read only. Care should be used when writing to the STATUS register as the ALU status bits will be updated upon completion of the write operation thereby leaving the STATUS register with a result that is different than intended. Therefore, it is recommended that only SETB, CLRB and PAGE instructions be used on this register.

STATUS							
7	6	5	4	3	2	1	0
PA2	PA1	PA0	TO	PD	Z	DC	C

Bits 7-5: Page select bits (PA2:PA0) *

000 = Page 0 ($000 - $1FF)
001 = Page 1 ($200 - $3FF)
010 = Page 2 ($400 - $5FF)
011 = Page 3 ($600 - $7FF)
100 = Page 4 ($800 - $9FF)
101 = Page 5 ($A00 - $BFF)
110 = Page 6 ($C00 - $DFF)
111 = Page 7 ($E00 - $FFF)

* For devices of less than 4 K code space, unused bits of PA2:PA0 may be used as general purpose read/write bits.

Bit 4: Time Out bit (TO)

Set (1) after power up, or executing a CLR !WDT or SLEEP instruction.
Cleared (0) after a watchdog time-out has occurred.

Bit 3: Power Down Bit (PD)

Set (1) after power up, or executing a CLR !WDT instruction.
Cleared (0) by a SLEEP instruction.

Bit 2: Zero Bit (Z)

Set (1) when the result of the most recent math operation was zero.
Cleared (0) when the result of the most recent math operation was non-zero.

Bit 1: Digit Carry (DC)

After an addition:

Set (1) = a carry from bit 4 has occurred
Clear (0) = no carry from bit 4 has occurred

After a subtraction:

Set (1) = no borrow from bit 4 has occurred
Clear (0) = a borrow from bit 4 has occurred

Bit 0: Carry (C)

After an addition:

Set (1) = a carry has occurred
Clear (0) = no carry has occurred

After a subtraction:

Set (1) = no borrow has occurred
Clear (0) = a borrow has occurred

The Carry flag also serves as the ninth bit in RL and RR instructions. We can examine the operation of each of these instructions to further clarify the behavior of the carry flag. Consider the RR instruction first. When an RR instruction is performed on a RAM byte, the data in the RAM byte is rotated *through* the carry flag.

Figure 23 - Rotate Right

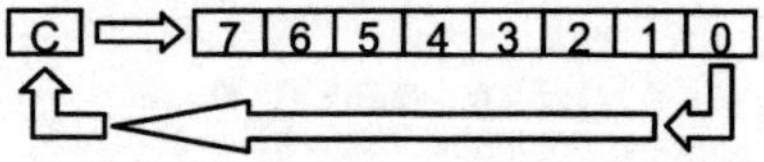

Similarly, when an RL instruction is performed on a RAM byte, the data in the RAM byte is rotated through the carry flag.

Figure 24 - Rotate Left

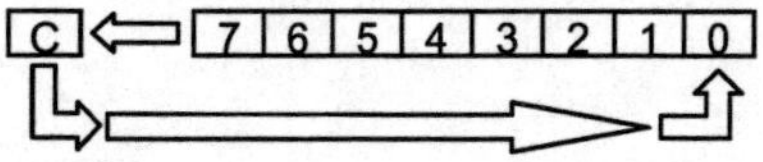

15.2.9 The FSR – File Select Register ($04)

The SX chip utilizes 12-bit op-codes. Instructions that specify a register as an operand can only express 5-bits of the register address. This means that only registers from $00 up to $1F can be accessed. The File Select Register (FSR) along with the 5-bit register operand is used to provide the ability to access registers beyond $1F. Figure 25 – **Global Register Addressing SX20/28/48/52 (direct)** shows how the FSR's upper three bits select one of eight RAM banks on the SX20/28. **Figure 26 – SX20/28 General Purpose Register Addressing (direct)** shows how the FSR's upper four bits select one of sixteen RAM banks on the SX48/52.

15 Appendix E: SX Data Sheet

Special function and general-purpose register addresses $00 - $0F are 'global' in that they can always be accessed regardless of the contents of the FSR. Special function register $07 (RC) is available as general purpose RAM in 20-pin SX packages. Special function registers $08 (RD) and $09 (RE) are available as general-purpose RAM in 20 and 28-pin SX packages.

15.2.10 Direct Addressing

Global registers can be directly accessed at any time but general-purpose registers can only be directly accessed within the current bank. The global registers are numbered $01 through $0F. **Figure 25 – Global Register Addressing SX 20/28/48/52 (direct)** shows how the Global Registers are addressed in the SX20/28 and the SX48/52. Simply specify the desired global register address in the fr operand (the register address operand) of instructions as shown below:

```
mov          $0F, #$55     ; move $55 to global register $0F
```

Figure 25 - Global Register Addressing SX20/28/48/52 (direct)

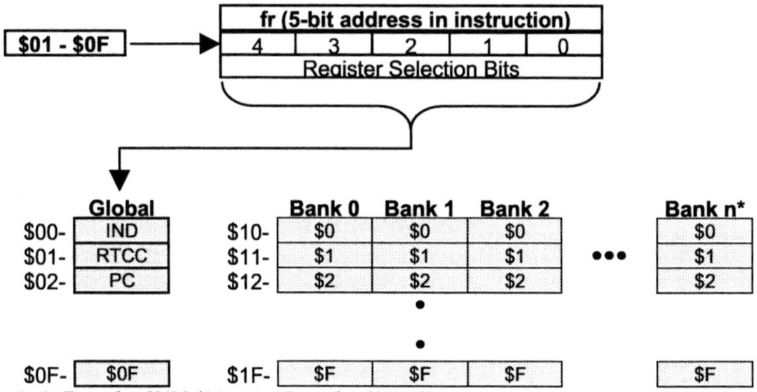

*n is 7 on the SX20/28. n is 15 on the SX48/52

General-purpose registers can only be accessed within one bank at a time. The general-purpose registers are numbered $10 through $1F. The active bank is controlled by the upper 3 bits of the FSR (SX20/28) as shown in **Figure 26 – SX20/28 General Purpose Register Addressing (direct)** or the upper 4 bits of the FSR (SX48/52) as shown in **Figure 27 – SX 48/52 General-Purpose Register Addressing (direct).**

Figure 26 - SX20/28 General Purpose Register Addressing (direct)

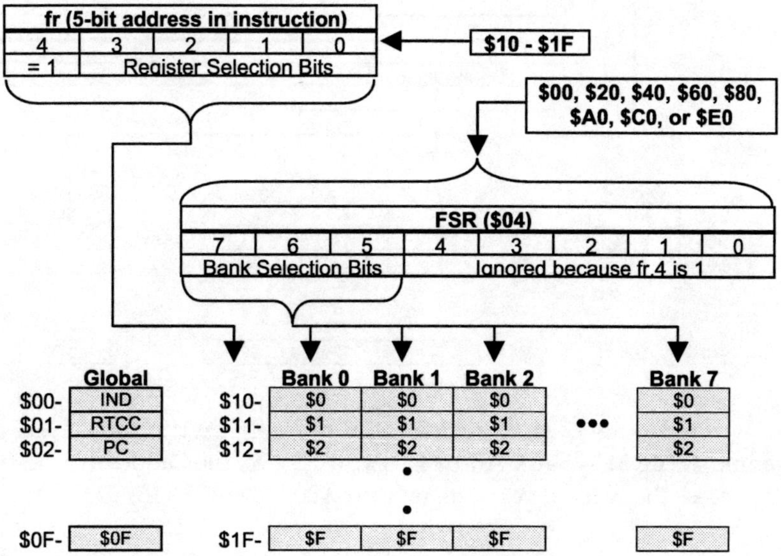

Figure 27 - SX48/52 General-Purpose Register addressing (direct)

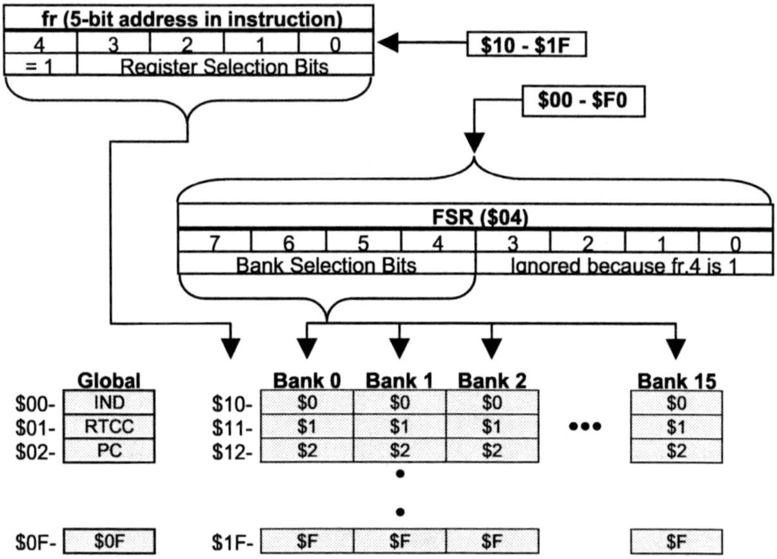

To ensure you are writing to the desired register you must first write the correct value to the FSR to select the proper bank. **Table 31 – Bank Addresses and FSR Values** and the code fragments will show you how to directly access the banked registers on the SX20/28 and SX48/52.

Table 31 - Bank Addresses and FSR Values

SX20/28		SX48/52	
Desired Bank	FSR Value	Desired Bank	FSR Value
0	$00	0	$00
1	$20	1	$10
2	$40	2	$20
3	$60	3	$30
4	$80	4	$40
5	$A0	5	$50
6	$C0	6	$60
7	$E0	7	$70
-		8	$80
-		9	$90
-		10	$A0
-		11	$B0
-		12	$C0
-		13	$D0
-		14	$E0
-		15	$F0

This example clears register $10 in banks 3 and 6 on the SX20/28:

```
mov     FSR, #$60    ; Select Bank 3
clr     $10          ; Clear register $10 on Bank 3
mov     FSR, #$C0    ; Select Bank 6
clr     $10          ; Clear register $10 on Bank 6
```

This example clears register $10 in banks 3 and 6 on the SX48/52:

```
mov     FSR, #$30    ; Select Bank 3
clr     $10          ; Clear register $10 on Bank 3
mov     FSR, #$60    ; Select Bank 6
clr     $10          ; Clear register $10 on Bank 6
```

15.2.11 Indirect Addressing

To access any register via indirect addressing, simply move the 8-bit address of the register you wish to access into the FSR and use IND ($00) as the operand.

Figure 28- SX20/28 Indirect register addressing

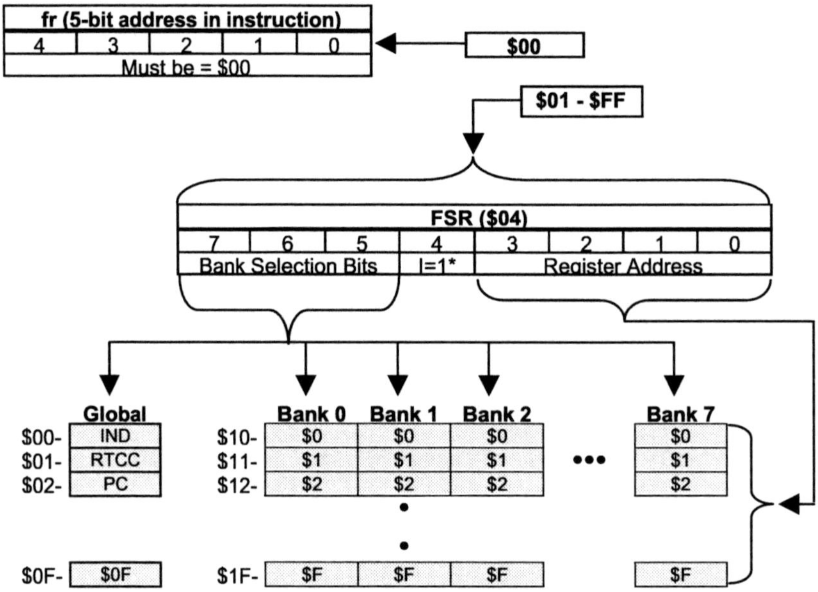

* FSR.4 must be 1 to access banked general purpose RAM, set FSR.4 = 0 for global RAM.

Figure 29 - SX48/52 Indirect register addressing

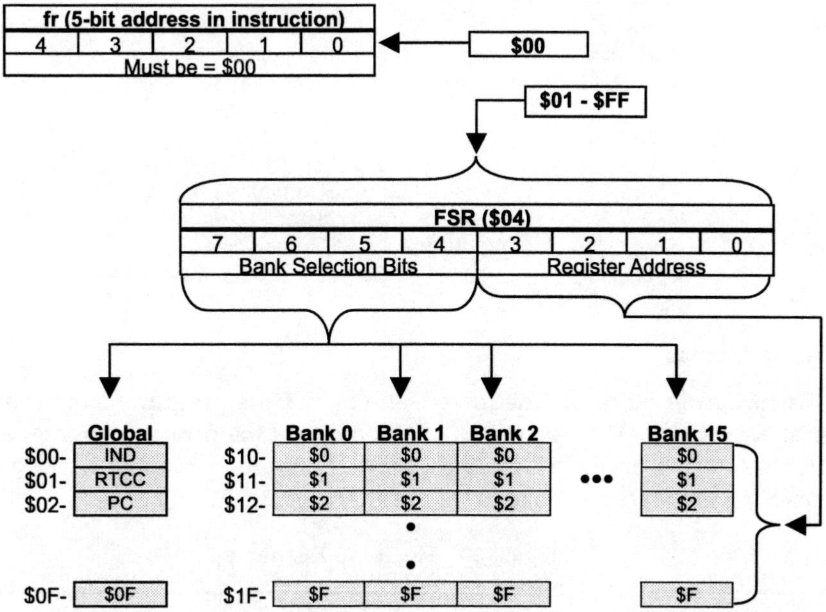

This example for the SX20/28 will clear every General Purpose RAM register on every bank using indirect addressing.

```
Init    mov  FSR, #$10        ; FSR = addr of 1st RAM Reg.
Loop    clr  IND              ; Clear register
        inc  FSR              ; Point to next register
        setb FSR.4            ; Keep us on G.P. RAM area
        cjne FSR, #$10, Loop  ; Repeat until all registers
                              ; have been cleared
```

15.2.12 The Bank Instruction

Often it is desirable to set the bank select bits of the FSR with one instruction cycle (the MOV FSR, #literal commands above take two cycles). The SX instruction set offers such an instruction called Bank. The Bank instruction sets the upper bits of the FSR to point to the RAM bank required. Note: *On the SX48/52, the BANK instruction only selects one of 8 banks in either the lower 8 or upper 8 banks. FSR.7 selects the lower or upper group of 8 banks. To select a bank, use MOV FSR, #literal or add an SETB FSR.7 instruction after the BANK instruction.* Here's an example of how to use the Bank instruction on the SX20/28:

```
Zero     EQU $00
One      EQU $30
Two      EQU $50
Three    EQU $70
Four     EQU $90
Five     EQU $B0
Six      EQU $D0
Seven    EQU $F0

bank     Three        ; Make FSR point to bank 3
clr      $10          ; Clear register $10 (in bank 3)
bank     Six          ; Make FSR point to bank 6
mov      $10,#1       ; Set register $10 (in bank 6) to 1
```

15.2.13 The Jump Instruction

When a JMP instruction is executed, the lower nine bits of the program counter are loaded with the address of the label specified. The upper two or three bits of the program counter are loaded with the page select bits, PA2:PA0, from the STATUS register. Therefore, care must be used to ensure the page select bits are pointing to the correct page *before* the jump occurs.

Figure 30 - The Jump Instruction

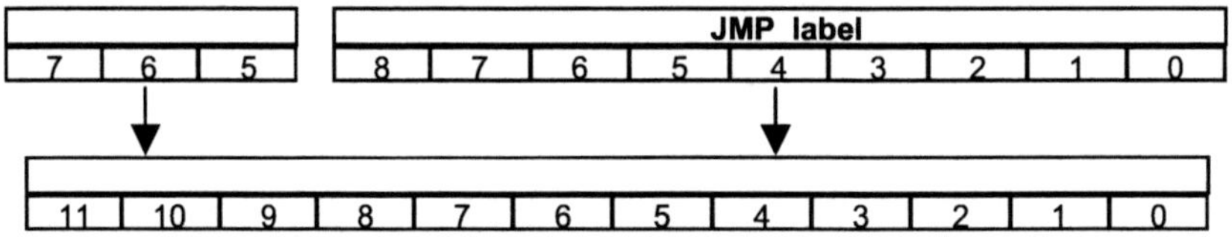

15.2.14 Jumping Across Pages

When a JMP instruction is executed and the intended destination is on a different page, you must set the page select bits to point to the desired page before the jump occurs. This can be done discretely with SETB and CLRB instructions or by writing a value to the STATUS register. The SX offers a single-cycle instruction called PAGE that sets the page select bits for you. See "Dealing with Code Pages" in Chapter 10.6 for more information. *NOTE: Using the @ symbol in the JMP instruction (JMP @label) will cause the assembler to insert the PAGE instruction before your JMP, during assembly.*

Figure 31 - Jumping Across Pages

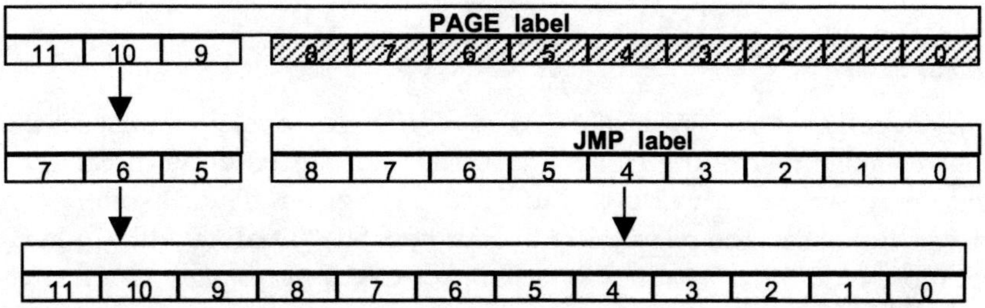

15.2.15 The Call Instruction

When a CALL instruction is executed, four things occur:

1) the current value of the program counter is incremented and pushed onto the top of the stack;
2) the lower eight bits of the address of the label are copied into the lower eight bits of the program counter
3) the ninth bit of the PC is cleared to zero
4) the page select bits of the STATUS register are copied into the upper bits of the PC. Since bit 8 is cleared, the call destination must *start* in the lower half of any page of code space. i.e. $00-$FF, $200-$2FF, $400-$4FF, etc.

Figure 32 - The Call Instruction

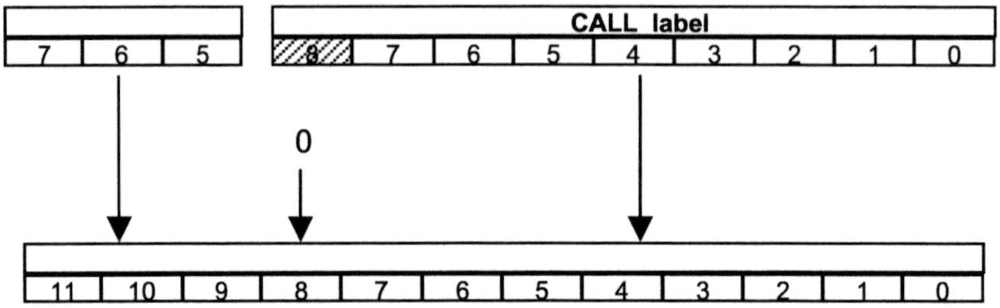

15.2.16 Calling Across Pages

When it is necessary to call a subroutine that exists on a different page, you must set the page select bits to point to the desired page before the call is executed. This can be done discretely using SETB and CLRB instructions or by writing a value to the STATUS register. The SX offers a new single-cycle instruction called PAGE that sets the page select bits for you. See "Dealing with Code Pages" in Chapter 7 for more information. *NOTE: Using the @ symbol in the CALL instruction (CALL @label) will cause the assembler to insert the PAGE instruction before your CALL, during assembly.*

Figure 33 - Calling Across Pages

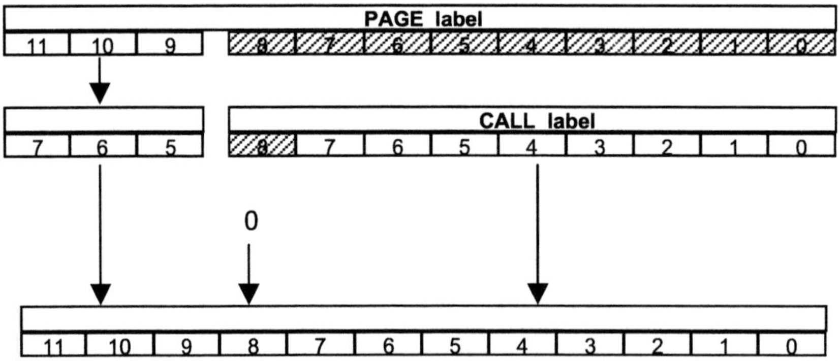

15.2.17 Returning from a subroutine

Subroutines are usually terminated with a return-type instruction. Before we discuss the different return instructions, we should describe the operation of the stack.

15.2.18 The Stack

The stack is an area of memory used to remember where to return to once a subroutine is complete. The stack is eight levels deep with the Stack Extend (STACKX) option set and two levels deep by default (*On SX48/52 devices, the stack is always eight levels deep*). That means it can remember the return addresses for subroutines nested up to eight levels. The following explanation assumes that the SX has the Stack Extend option selected. The stack is capable of two operations; push and pop. The stack behaves like a plate holder in a salad buffet. A push is similar to placing a plate on the top of the stack and a pop is similar to removing a plate from the top of the stack.

15.2.19 The Push

When a subroutine is called, the return address is pushed onto the stack. Specifically, each address in the stack is moved to the next lower level in order to make room for the new address to be stored. Stack 1 gets the value that was in the program counter. Stack 8 is overwritten with what was in Stack 7. Consequently, the previous contents of Stack 8 are lost forever.

Figure 34 - The Push

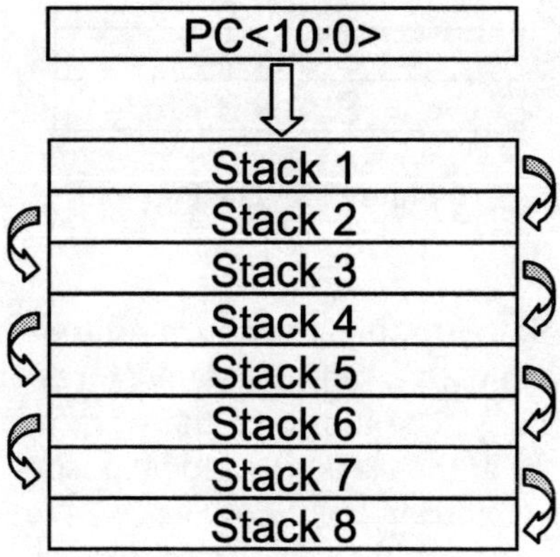

15.2.20 The Pop

When a return instruction is executed, the stack is popped. Specifically, the content of Stack 1 is copied to the program counter and the content of each address in the stack is copied to the next higher level. Stack 1 gets the value that was in Stack 2, etc. until Stack 7 is overwritten with the contents of Stack 8. Consequently, the contents that were in Stack 8 are now duplicated in Stack 7.

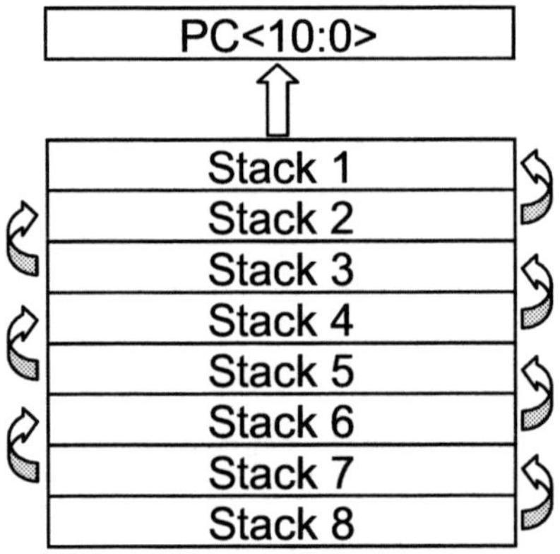

Figure 35 - The Pop

15.2.21 Stack Overflow

As mentioned before, the stack can store up to eight return addresses (with Stack Extend on), or up to two return addresses by default. With each push, the stack stores another address. When the stack is full, the next push results in an overflow. The first time the stack is pushed into an overflow condition, the first address pushed is lost forever. If the stack were to be pushed again, the second address pushed would be lost also. A stack overflow condition inevitably leads to unintentional infinite loops or bizarre looping actions in your program. Care should be taken to ensure a stack overflow does not ever occur.

15.2.22 Stack Underflow

When the stack is popped more times than it has been pushed, a stack underflow occurs. Since a stack underflow causes unknown addresses to be stored in PC, a program may perform bizarre looping actions, such as a jump to unused program memory.

15.2.23 Returns

There are five different return instructions available on the SX. The RET (return) instruction simply pops the stack thereby setting the program counter to the instruction that followed the call. The RETW (return with literal in w) instruction behaves the same way but loads W with the literal value specified. RETP pops the stack and updates the page select bits to point to the page returned to. RETI pops the stack and the special shadow registers for W, STATUS, and the FSR, which were preserved during interrupt handling. RETIW behaves the same as RETI but also compensates the RTCC by adding the value in W to the RTCC.

15.3 Port Configuration Registers

15.3.1 Port A Registers

There are three registers used to configure the I/O pins of Port A. The TRIS_A register configures the data direction of the Port A pins as input or output. The LVL_A register configures the input pins as TTL or CMOS voltage level. The PLP_A register enables/disables pull up resistors on Port A input pins. To access these registers you must first write a particular value to the MODE register. Please refer toTable **32 – SX20/28 Mode Register** to find the values required in the MODE register to access the following Port A Registers. *Note: All the bits in the following registers are set to '1' on power up.*

15.3.1.1 TRIS_A – Data Direction Register

TRIS_A							
7	6	5	4	3	2	1	0
-	-	-	-	RA3	RA2	RA1	RA0

A bit set to '1' in this register sets the corresponding I/O port pin to input (high z) mode.
A bit set to '0' in this register sets the corresponding I/O port pin to output mode.

15.3.1.2 LVL_A - TTL/CMOS Select Register

LVL_A							
7	6	5	4	3	2	1	0
-	-	-	-	RA3	RA2	RA1	RA0

A bit set to '1' in this register sets the input level of the corresponding port pin to TTL.
A bit set to '0' in this register sets the input level of the corresponding port pin to CMOS.

15.3.1.3 PLP_A – Pull-Up Resistor Enable Register

PLP_A							
7	6	5	4	3	2	1	0
-	-	-	-	RA3	RA2	RA1	RA0

A bit set to '1' in this register disables the weak pull-up resistor on the corresponding port pin. A bit set to '0' in this register enables the weak pull-up resistor on the corresponding port pin.

15.3.2 Port B Registers

There are eight registers used to configure the I/O pins of Port B. The TRIS_B register configures the data direction of the Port B pins as input or output. The LVL_B register configures the input pins as TTL or CMOS voltage level. The PLP_B register enables/disables pull up resistors on Port B input pins. The ST_B register enables/disables the Schmitt-Trigger inputs on Port B input pins. The WKEN_B register enables/disables the multi-input wake up for interrupts on Port B input pins. The WKED_B register selects rising/falling edge detection on Port B input pins. The WKPND_B register contains the state of the MIWU pins. The CMP_B registers configures and provides the results from the comparator pins. To access these registers you must first write a particular value to the MODE register. Please refer to Table 32 – **SX20/28 Mode Register** to find the values required in the MODE register to access the Port B Registers. *Note: All the bits in the following registers are set to '1' on power up.*

15.3.2.1 TRIS_B – Data Direction Register

TRIS_B							
7	6	5	4	3	2	1	0
RB7	RB6	RB5	RB4	RB3	RB2	RB1	RB0

A bit set to '1' in this register sets the corresponding I/O port pin to input (high z) mode.
A bit set to '0' in this register sets the corresponding I/O port pin to output mode.

15.3.2.2 LVL_B - TTL/CMOS Select Register

LVL_B							
7	6	5	4	3	2	1	0
RB7	RB6	RB5	RB4	RB3	RB2	RB1	RB0

A bit set to '1' in this register sets the input level of the corresponding port pin to TTL.
A bit set to '0' in this register sets the input level of the corresponding port pin to CMOS.

15.3.2.3 PLP_B – Pull-Up Resistor Enable Register

PLP_B							
7	6	5	4	3	2	1	0
RB7	RB6	RB5	RB4	RB3	RB2	RB1	RB0

A bit set to '1' in this register disables the weak pull-up resistor on the corresponding port pin. A bit set to '0' in this register enables the weak pull-up resistor on the corresponding port pin.

15.3.2.4 ST_B – Schmitt-Trigger Enable Register

ST_B							
7	6	5	4	3	2	1	0
RB7	RB6	RB5	RB4	RB3	RB2	RB1	RB0

A bit set to '1' in this register disables the Schmitt-Trigger input on the corresponding port pin. A bit set to '0' in this register enables the Schmitt-Trigger input on the corresponding port pin.

15.3.2.5 WKEN_B – Wake Up Enable Register

WKEN_B							
7	6	5	4	3	2	1	0
RB7	RB6	RB5	RB4	RB3	RB2	RB1	RB0

A bit set to '1' in this register disables the multi-input wake up for the corresponding port pin. A bit set to '0' in this register enables the multi-input wake up for the corresponding port pin.

15.3.2.6 WKED_B – Wake Up Edge Select Register

WKED_B							
7	6	5	4	3	2	1	0
RB7	RB6	RB5	RB4	RB3	RB2	RB1	RB0

A bit set to '1' in this register selects falling edge detection for the corresponding port pin.
A bit set to '0' in this register selects rising edge detection for the corresponding port pin.

15.3.2.7 WKPND_B – MIWU Pending Register

WKPND_B							
7	6	5	4	3	2	1	0
RB7	RB6	RB5	RB4	RB3	RB2	RB1	RB0

A bit set to '1' in this register indicates a rising or falling edge was detected for the corresponding port pin. A bit set to '0' in this register indicates no edge was detected on the corresponding port pin since that bit was last cleared.

15.3.2.8 CMP_B – Comparator Enable Register

CMP_B							
7	6	5	4	3	2	1	0
EN	OE	Rsvd	Rsvd	Rsvd	Rsvd	Rsvd	RES

EN - Comparator Enable, 0 = enabled, 1 = disabled
OE - Comparator Output Enable, 0 = enabled, 1 = disabled
Rsvd - Reserved for future use
RES - Comparator Result (EN must = 0)

15.3.3 Port C Registers

There are four registers used to configure the I/O pins of Port C. The TRIS_C register configures the data direction of the Port C pins as input or output. The LVL_C register configures the input pins as TTL or CMOS voltage level. The PLP_C register enables/disables pull up resistors on Port C input pins. The ST_C register enables/disables the Schmitt-Trigger inputs on Port C input pins. To access these registers you must first write a particular value to the MODE register. Please refer to Table **32 – SX20/28 Mode Register** to find the values required in the MODE register to access the Port C Registers. *Note: All the bits in the following registers are set to '1' on power up.*

15.3.3.1 TRIS_C – Data Direction Register

TRIS_C							
7	6	5	4	3	2	1	0
RC7	RC6	RC5	RC4	RC3	RC2	RC1	RC0

A bit set to '1' in this register sets the corresponding I/O port pin to input (high z) mode.
A bit set to '0' in this register sets the corresponding I/O port pin to output mode.

15.3.3.2 LVL_C - TTL/CMOS Select Register

LVL_C							
7	6	5	4	3	2	1	0
RC7	RC6	RC5	RC4	RC3	RC2	RC1	RC0

A bit set to '1' in this register sets the input level of the corresponding port pin to TTL.
A bit set to '0' in this register sets the input level of the corresponding port pin to CMOS.

15.3.3.3 PLP_C – Pull-Up Resistor Enable Register

PLP_C							
7	6	5	4	3	2	1	0
RC7	RC6	RC5	RC4	RC3	RC2	RC1	RC0

A bit set to '1' in this register disables the weak pull-up resistor on the corresponding port pin. A bit set to '0' in this register enables the weak pull-up resistor on the corresponding port pin.

15.3.3.4 ST_C – Schmitt-Trigger Enable Register

ST_C							
7	6	5	4	3	2	1	0
RC7	RC6	RC5	RC4	RC3	RC2	RC1	RC0

A bit set to '1' in this register disables the Schmitt-Trigger input on the corresponding port pin. A bit set to '0' in this register enables the Schmitt-Trigger input on the corresponding port pin.

15.3.4 Port D and E Registers (SX48/52)

The SX48/52 devices have two additional 8 bit ports, called Port D and Port E. Their configuration registers are similar to the Port C configuration registers. Please refer to chapter 15.3.3 for the details.

15.4 Control registers

There are three registers that configure the SX: MODE, OPTION, and Fuses. These registers allow the user to configure the SX in many ways. MODE and OPTION are run-time readable and writable while Fuses is written to only at program time.

15.4.1 Mode register (SX20/28)

The MODE register (simply called M in SX-Key mnemonics) is a run-time readable and writable register used to select the configuration registers for port operations.

MODE							
7	6	5	4	3	2	1	0
0	0	0	0	M3	M2	M1	M0

When a port configuration instruction is executed, such as MOV !RA, #1, the value of the MODE determines exactly which type of port configuration register will be written to. The right 4 bits in this register are set to '1' on power up. Below is an example detailing how the MODE register is used.

```
mov     M, #$0F      ; Set up MODE for Direction configuration
mov     !RA, #$03    ; RA3:RA2 = Outputs, RA1:RA0 = Inputs
mov     M, #$0E      ; Set up MODE for Pull-Up configuration
mov     !RA, #$01    ; RA3:RA1 = Normal, RA0 = Pull-up enabled
mov     M, #$0D      ; Set up MODE for TTL/CMOS configuration
mov     !RA, #$02    ; RA3, RA2, RA0 = TTL, RA1 = CMOS
```

Table 32 – SX20/28 Mode Register, below, defines the allowed mode values and their functions for the SX20/28 devices. The gray areas are undefined at this time.

Table 32 – SX20/28 Mode Register

SX20/28 MODE (m) Register and mov !r?, W			
m	mov !ra, w	mov !rb, w	mov !rc, w
$0F	write TRIS_A	write TRIS_B	write TRIS_C
$0E	write PLP_A	write PLP_B	write PLP_C
$0D	write LVL_A	write LVL_B	write LVL_C
$0C		write ST_B	write ST_C
$0B		write WKEN_B	
$0A		write WKED_B	
$09		swap W with WKPEN_B	
$08		swap W with COMP_B	
$07…$00			

15.4.2 Mode register (SX48/52)

Similar to the SX20/28, instructions like mov !ra, w are used to access the control registers with the MODE register previously set to a value to select the correct register type. **Table 33 - SX48/52 Mode Register**, shows the possible values for the MODE register. The gray areas are undefined.

Table 33 - SX48/52 Mode Register

SX48/52 MODE (m) Register and mov !r?, w					
m	mov !ra, w	mov !rb, w	mov !rc, w	mov !rd, w	mov !re, w
$00		read T1CPL	read T2PL		
$01		read T1CPH	read T2CPH		
$02		read T1R2CML	read T2R2CML		
$03		read T1R2CMH	read T2R2CMH		
$04		read T1R1CML	read T2R1CML		
$05		read T1R1CMH	read T2R1CMH		
$06		read T1CNTB	read T2CNTB		
$07		read T1CNTA	read T2CNTA		
$08		exchange CMP_B			
$09		exchange WKPND_B			
$0a		write WKED_B			
$0b		write WKEN_B			
$0c		read ST_B	read ST_C	read ST_D	read ST_E
$0d	read LVL_A	read LVL_B	read LVL_C	read LVL_D	read LVL_E
$0e	read PLP_A	read PLP_B	read PLP_C	read PLP_D	read PLP_E
$0f	read TRIS_A	read TRIS_B	read TRIS_C	read TRIS_D	read TRIS_E
$10		clear Timer 1	clear Timer 2		
$11					
$12		write T1R2CML	write T2R2CML		
$13		write T1R2CMH	write T2R2CMH		
$14		write T1R1CML	write T2R1CML		
$15		write T1R1CMH	write T2R1CMH		
$16		write T1CNTB	write T2CNTB		
$17		write T1CNTA	write T2CNTA		
$18		exchange CMP_B			
$19		exchange WKPND_B			
$1a		write WKED_B			
$1b		write WKEN_B			
$1c		write ST_B	write ST_C	write ST_D	write ST_E
$1d	write LVL_A	write LVL_B	write LVL_C	write LVL_D	write LVL_E
$1e	write PLP_A	write PLP_B	write PLP_C	write PLP_D	write PLP_E
$1f	write TRIS_A	write TRIS_B	write TRIS_C	write TRIS_D	write TRIS_E

Abbreviations: T1CPH, T2CPH: Timer 1/2 capture, high byte. T1CPL, T2CPL: Timer 1/2 capture, low byte. T1R1CMH, T2R1CMH: Timer 1/2 register R1, high byte. T1R1CML, T2R1CML: Timer 1/2 register R1, low byte. T1R2CMH, T2R2CMH: Timer 1/2 register R2, high byte. T1R2CML, T2R2CML: Timer 1/2 register R2, low byte.

15.4.3 Option

The OPTION register is a run-time writable register used to configure the RTCC and the Watchdog Timer. The size of this register is affected by the OPTIONX device setting.

OPTION							
7	6	5	4	3	2	1	0
RTW	RTI	RTS	RTE	PSA	PS2	PS1	PS0

When OPTION Extend = 0, bits 7 and 6 are implemented.
When OPTION Extend = 1, bits 7 and 6 read as '1's.

RTW - If = 0, register $01 is W
If = 1, register $01 is RTCC
RTI - If = 0, RTCC roll-over interrupt is enabled
If = 1, RTCC roll-over interrupt is disabled
RTS - If = 0, RTCC increments on internal instruction cycle
If = 1, RTCC increments on transition of RTCC pin
RTE - If = 0, RTCC increments on low-to-high transition
If = 1, RTCC increments on high-to-low transition
PSA - If = 0, prescaler is assigned to RTCC, divide rate determined by PS0-PS2 bits
If = 1, prescaler is assigned to WDT, and divide rate on RTCC is 1:1

Figure 36 - Prescaler Division Ratios

PS2, PS1, PS0	RTCC Divide Rate	Watchdog Timer Divide Rate
000	1:2	1:1
001	1:4	1:2
010	1:8	1:4
011	1:16	1:8
100	1:32	1:16
101	1:64	1:32
110	1:128	1:64
111	1:256	1:128

15.4.4 Fuse Registers

The Fuse registers are accessible only at program time. The SX-Key Development System Software provides a convenient interface that is easy to use to customize the SX. You may use the predefined device directives in your source code to specify the bits in the Fuses register. See "Device Directive" in Chapter 7.3.1 for additional information.

15.5 Interrupts

15.5.1 Description

Sometimes a particular task or event must have the immediate attention of the processor. An interrupt is a means to accomplish this. In theory, the processor stops whatever it was doing and immediately begins executing code located at a special location called the Interrupt Vector. Once the code located at the Interrupt Vector task has completed, the processor returns to where it was before the interruption occurred.

In reality, several things must occur in addition to the aforementioned to ensure proper operation of the interrupt and the rest of the program. For one thing, consider the likely possibility that the interrupt occurred when the W register held a number the main program was using for a calculation. More than likely, the interrupt service routine will use the W register for its purposes too. When the processor finishes the interrupt service routine and returns to what it was doing before, the W register will hold a different value than what it held before the interrupt occurred. This can lead to bizarre program execution. In addition to the W register, the Status and FSR registers must be 'preserved' across an interrupt.

Traditionally, these issues were dealt with by software within the interrupt service routine. The engineers at Ubicom had the foresight to take the burden off the programmer and put it in the chip where it belongs.

15.5.2 The Specifics

When an interrupt occurs in an SX chip, the PC, STATUS, FSR, and W registers are saved in special shadow locations, and additional interrupts ignored. The program counter is loaded with $00, (The Interrupt Vector), and the top three bits of the STATUS register, (PA2:PA0) are cleared to $0. When the interrupt service routine has completed and the 'RETI' instruction is executed, the PC, STATUS, FSR, and W registers are restored and the interrupt is re-enabled. Since this occurs automatically, your interrupt service routine does not have to waste any valuable time copying several registers back and forth.

15.5.3 RTCC Interrupt

The SX chip offers one internal interrupt called the RTCC rollover. If enabled, when the RTCC increments from $FF to $00, an interrupt will be generated. The latency, or response delay, will be exactly three instruction cycles in Turbo Mode, and exactly eight cycles in Non-Turbo mode. When the interrupt is complete, there will be a three-cycle delay (Turbo mode) or an eight-cycle delay (Non-Turbo mode) before main code begins executing. This is due to the pipeline. Whenever an instruction is executed and, because of the instruction, the program counter is changed, the pipeline must be flushed and refilled. See "RTCC Rollover Interrupts" in Chapter 10.4.1 for more information.

In addition, the SX48/52 devices also allow interrupts on certain timer events, like overflow, compare match, and input capture.

15.5.4 RB0-RB7 Interrupt

The SX offers eight sources of external interrupts; a change of state on any of RB0 – RB7 can generate an interrupt. These can be individually configured via the WKEN_B and WKED_B configuration registers. The latency, or response delay, will be five cycles in Turbo mode and ten cycles in Non-Turbo mode. See "Wake-Up (Interrupt) on Edge Detect" in Chapter 10.2.5 for more information.

15.6 Peripherals

15.6.1 Oscillator Driver

The SX chips offer a configurable oscillator driver that supports five types of oscillators:

LP: Low Power Oscillator
XT: Crystal or Resonator
HS: High Speed Crystal or Resonator
RC: Resistor/Capacitor (external)
IRC: Resistor/Capacitor (internal)

An external clock source can also be used to drive the OSC1 pin (leaving the OSC2 pin disconnected) as in Figure 39 – **SX with External Clock.**

15.6.1.1 LP, XT and HS Mode

In XT, LP, and HS modes, a crystal or ceramic resonator can be connected to the SX chip as in **Figure 37 - SX with External Crystal** or in **Figure 38 - SX with External Ceramic Resonator.** The SX oscillator driver design requires the use of a parallel cut crystal. Use of a series cut crystal may give a frequency out of the crystal manufacturer's specifications. The values of the components can be determined from **Table 34 – External Component Selection for Crystals**, below. Please note that some ceramic resonators have internal capacitors so that no external capacitors are required.

Figure 37 - SX with External Crystal

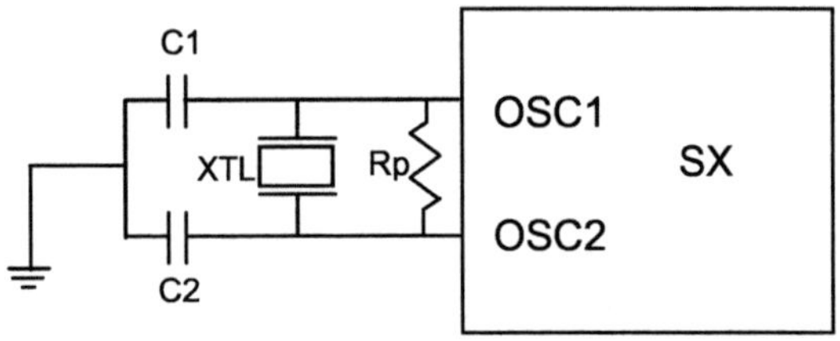

Table 34 – External Component Selection for Crystals (Vdd = 5V)

OSC Setting	Crystal Frequency	C1	C2	Rp
OSCXT1	4 MHz	15 pF	22 pF	1 MΩ
OSCXT2	8 MHz	56 pF	33 pF	1 MΩ
OSCXT2	20 MHz	33 pF	22 pF	1 MΩ
OSCXT2	32 MHz	15 pF	22 pF	1 MΩ
OSCHS1	50 MHz	15 pF	15 pF	1 MΩ

Figure 38 - SX with External Ceramic Resonator

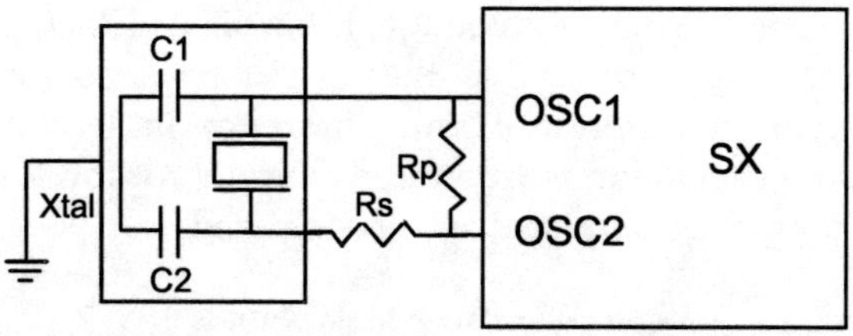

Table 35 - Component Selection for Murata Ceramic Resonators (Vdd = 5.0 V)

OSC Setting	Frequency	Resonator Part Number	C1	C2	Rp
OSCXT2	4 MHz	CSA4.00MG	30 pF	30 pF	1 MΩ
OSCXT2	4 MHz	CST4.00MGW	30 pF *	30 pF *	1 MΩ
OSCXT2	4 MHz	CSTCC4.00G0H6	47 pF *	47 pF *	1 MΩ
OSCXT2	8 MHz	CSA8.00MTZ	30 pF	30 pF	1 MΩ
OSCXT2	8 MHz	CST8.00MTW	30 pF *	30 pF *	1 MΩ
OSCXT2	8 MHz	CSTCC8.00MG0H6	47 pF *	47 pF *	1 MΩ
OSCXT2	20 MHz	CSA20.00MXZ040	5 pF	5 pF	1 MΩ
OSCXT2	20 MHz	CST20.00MXW0H1	5 pF *	5 pF *	1 MΩ
OSCXT2	20 MHz	CSACV20.00MXJ040	5 pF	5 pF	22 kΩ
OSCXT2	20 MHz	CSTCV20.00MXJ0H1	5 pF *	5 pF *	22 kΩ
OSCHS1	33 MHz	CSA33.00MXJ040	5 pF	5 pF	1 MΩ
OSCHS1	33 MHz	CST33.00MXW040	5 pF *	5 pF *	1 MΩ
OSCHS1	33 MHz	CSACV33.00MXJ040	5 pF	5 pF	1 MΩ
OSCHS1	33 MHz	CSTCV33.00MXJ040	5 pF *	5 pF *	1 MΩ
OSCHS2	50 MHz	CSA50.00MXZ040	15 pF	15 pF	10 kΩ
OSCHS2	50 MHz	CST50.00MXW0H3	15 pF *	15 pF *	10 kΩ
OSCHS2	50 MHz	CSACV50.00MXJ040	15 pF	15 pF	10 kΩ
OSCHS2	50 MHz	CSTCV50.00MXJ0H3	15 pF *	15 pF *	10 kΩ

* Capacitors built in to resonator
Note: Rs is zero for all configurations.

Figure 39 - SX with External System Clock

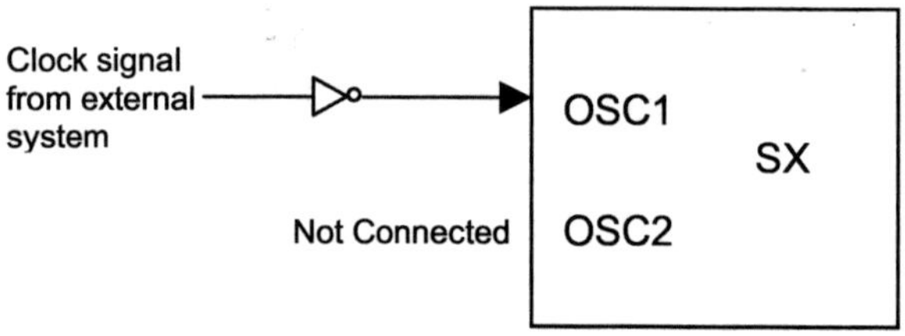

15.6.1.2 External RC Mode

For timing insensitive applications, the RC device option offers additional cost savings. The RC oscillator frequency is a function of the supply voltage, the resistor (Rext) and capacitor (Cext) values, and the operating temperature. In addition to this, the oscillator frequency will vary from unit to unit due to normal process variation. Furthermore, the difference in lead frame capacitance between package types will also affect the oscillation frequency, especially for low Cext values. Variation due to tolerance of external R and C components must also be considered.

Figure 40 - External RC Mode

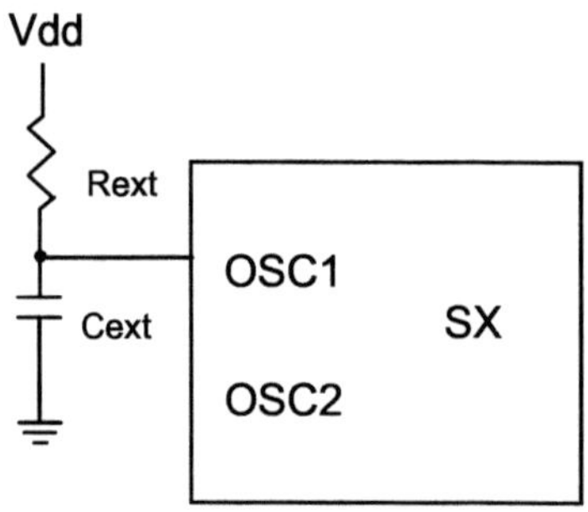

Figure 40 - External RC Mode shows the RC connections to the SX. For Rext values below 2.2kΩ, the oscillator operation may become unstable, or stop completely. For very high Rext values (e.g. 1 MΩ) the oscillator becomes sensitive to noise, humidity and leakage. The recommended Rext value is 3kΩ to 100kΩ.

Although the oscillator will operate with no external capacitor (Cext = 0 pF), using values above 20 pF is recommended for noise and stability reasons. With little external capacitance, the oscillation frequency can vary dramatically due to changes in external capacitance, such as PCB trace capacitance or package lead frame capacitance.

15.6.1.3 Internal RC Mode

The SX offers an internal 4 MHz RC oscillator for timing insensitive operations. Using the internal oscillator reduces external component count and system cost. The internal oscillator is configured via the OSC4MHZ through OSC32KHZ device settings and the IRC Calibration settings. The SX-Key Development software's Configure dialog allows you to select the internal RC oscillator calibration factor (Slow, 4 MHz or Fast). When using SASM, a directive (IRC_CAL) is also available, allowing source code to have the proper fuse configuration embedded within it.

The IRC_4MHZ settings is used to adjust the operation of the internal RC oscillator to make it operate within the target frequency range of 4 MHz ± 8%. The devices leave the factory untrimmed.

When using SASM, the SX-Key software automatically performs a calibration when the source code contains the *IRC_CAL IRC_4MHZ* directive, and sets the calibration bits accordingly when it downloads a program to the SX device.

Please note that the calibration process takes extra programming time. Therefore, when you don't intend to use the internal RC oscillator, place an *IRC_CAL IRC_SLOW* or *IRC_CAL IRC_FAST* directive in your source code to always set the calibration bits to the lowest or highest value. In this case, the auto calibrate step will be skipped.

15 Appendix E: SX Data Sheet

16 Index

_

_SASM pre-defined constant, 72

=

= directive, 47

A

ADD instruction, 123
ADDB instruction, 123
Addressing, direct, 156
Addressing, indirect, 160
AND instruction, 123
Architecture, SX, 150
Assemble, 23
Assembler directives, 45
Assembler options, 28
Assembler selection, 28
Assembly code box, 33
Assembly program, structure of, 44

B

Backup files, 28, 73
BANK instruction, 124, 161
BANKS option, 48
Binary operators, 71
BOR options, 48
Branching across pages, 105
BREAK directive, 47
Breakpoints, 37
Brownout selection, 40

C

C bit, 155
CALL across pages, 164
CALL instruction, 124, 163
Calling across pages, 106
Capture/Compare mode, 98
Carry bit, 155
CARRYX option, 48
CASE directive, 47
Ceramic oscillator, 176
CJA instruction, 124
CJAE instruction, 125
CJB instruction, 125
CJBE instruction, 125
CJE instruction, 126
CJNE instruction, 126
CLC instruction, 126
Clear error display, 23
Clock, 176
Clock control dialog, 25
Clock, external source, 178
Close file, 22
CLR instruction, 127
CLRB instruction, 127
CLZ instruction, 127
CMOS level, 90
CMP_B, 170
COM port, configuration of, 16
Comments, 45
Comments, colored, 29
Comparator, 95
Conditional assembly, 53, 54
Configure dialog, 25
Configure window, 28
Control registers, 171
Copy text, 23
Create a file, 21
Crystal oscillator, 176
CSA instruction, 127
CSAE instruction, 128
CSB instruction, 128
CSBE instruction, 129
CSE instruction, 129
CSNE instruction, 130
Cut text, 22

D

Data tables, 103
Data types, 72
DC bit, 155
Debug window, 34
Debugger, 31
Debugger, modifying registers, 36
Debugger, reentering, 24
Debugger, starting, 24
DEC instruction, 130
DECSZ instruction, 130
Device control dialog, 25
DEVICE directive, 48
DEVICE directive, Parallax assembler, 79
Device window, 39
Digit carry bit, 155
Direct addressing, 156
Direction configuration, 88
Directives, 45
Directives, Parallax assembler, 79
DJNZ instruction, 131
Download program, 24
Downloading to the SX, 17
DS directive, 51
DW directive, 51

E

Edge detection, 92
Edit - Clear Errors, 23
Edit - Copy, 23
Edit - Cut, 22
Edit - Debug, 24
Edit - Debug (reenter), 24
Edit - Find, 23
Edit - Find Next, 23
Edit - Find/Replace, 23
Edit - Go to Line Number, 23
Edit - Paste, 23

Edit - Redo, 22
Edit - Run, 24
Edit - Undo, 22
Edit - View List, 25
Edit menu, 22
Editor, 20
Editor selection, 29
Editor, shortcut keys, 21
END directive, 51
ENDM directive, 63
EQU directive, 47
ERROR directive, 52
Error display, clearing, 23
Error line, jump to option, 30
Error messages, Parallax assembler, 81
Error, background color, 30
Errors, SASM, 74
Exit the editor, 22
EXITM directive, 63
EXPAND directive, 63
Expression operators, 71
Expressions, 70
External event coounter, 98

F

File - Close, 22
File - Exit, 22
File - New, 21
File - Open, 21
File - Print, 22
File - Reopen, 22
File - Save, 22
File - Save As, 22
File menu, 21
File select register (FSR), 155
Files created by SASM, 73
Find and replace, 23
Find next, 23
Find text, 23
Find window, 26
Find/Replace window, 27
Formal parameters, 64
Formal parameters by count, 67
Formal parameters by name, 68
FREQ directive, 52
FSR, 155
Fuse registers, 174

G

General-purpose registers, 157
Global registers, 156
Go to line, 23
Goto Line Number window, 27

H

Help - About, 25
Help - Contents, 25
Help menu, 25

I

ID directive, 53
IF{N}DEF…ELSE…ENDIF, 54
IF…ELSE…ENDIF, 53
IFBD option, 48
IJNZ instruction, 131
INC instruction, 131
INCLUDE directive, 55
INCSZ instruction, 131
IND register, 153
Indirect addressing, 160
Installation of the software, 15
Instruction pipeline, 151
Instruction set, 111
Instructions, multi-word, 116
Instructions, quick reference, 118
Instructions, single word, 114
Interrupt latency, 99
Interrupt on edge detect, 93
Interrupt queuing, 99
Interrupt routine size, 99
Interrupt timing, 101
Interrupt vector, 99
Interrupt, auto-disable, 99
Interrupt, real time, 99
Interrupt, RTCC, 99
Interrupts, 99
Interrupts, multiple, 100
Interrupts, RTCC-rollover, 100
Interrupts, wake up, 103
IRC calibration, 179
IREAD instruction, 132

J

JB instruction, 132
JC instruction, 132
JMP across pages, 163
JMP instruction, 132, 162
JNB instruction, 133
JNC instruction, 133
JNZ instruction, 133
Jump tables, 106
Jump to Breakpoint button, 36
Jump to Code button, 36
Jump to Main button, 36
Jump to Next Run button, 36
Jump to Reset Line button, 36
JZ instruction, 133

K

Keywords, boldfaced, 29
Keywords, colored, 29

L

Labels, 69
Labels, local, 69
List file, 73
List file window, 35
List file, viewing, 25
LIST Q directive, 74
Load Hex, 41
LOCAL directive, 63
Local labels, 29, 69
Logic Level, 90
LVL_A, 167
LVL_B, 168
LVL_C, 170

M

M register, 173
MACRO directive, 62
Macro invocation, 65
Macro label, 70
Macros, 62
Macros, examples, 66
Macros, formal parameters, 64
Macros, formal parameters by count, 67
Macros, formal parameters by name, 68
Macros, parameters, 62
Macros, quoting, 65
Macros, token pasting, 65
Map file, 73
MODE instruction, 134
MODE register, 171, 173
Modifying register contents, 36
MOV instruction, 135
MOVB instruction, 136
MOVSZ instruction, 136
Multi-Funtion timers, 96
Multiple interrupts, 100

N

New file, 21
NOCASE directive, 47
NOEXPAND directive, 63
NOP instruction, 136
NOT instruction, 137

O

Object file, 73
Open file, 21
Operators in expressions, 71
Operators, binary, 71
Operators, unary, 71
OPTION register, 174
Options selection, 40
OPTIONX setting, 48
OR instruction, 137
ORG directive, 57
OSC options, 48
Oscillator driver, 176
Oscillator selection, 40

P

PAGE instruction, 137
Page select bits, 154
Parallax assembler, 79
Parallax web site, 3
Paste text, 23
PC register, 153
PD bit, 154
Pins option, 48
PLP_A, 167
PLP_B, 168
PLP_C, 171
Poll (debugger), 34
Pop, 166
Port A registers, 167
Port B registers, 168
Port C registers, 170
Port configuration, 87
Port D registers, 171
Port direction, 88
Port E registers, 171
Power down bit, 154
Print window, 25
Printing, 22
Program button, 40
Program counter, setting the, 37
Program download, 24
PROTECT option, 48
Pull-Up resistors, 89
Push, 165
PWM mode, 97

Q

Quick start, 17
Quit (debugger), 34
Quoting, 65

R

RB0-RB7 interrupt, 176
RC oscillator, external, 178
RC oscillator, internal, 179
Reading and verifying, 40
Read-Modify-Write, 151
Redo, 22
Register map, 151
Registers window, 31
Reopen file, 22
Repeating code, 58
REPT directive, 58
Reserved words, Parallax assembler, 84
Reserved words, SASM, 78
Reset (debugger), 34
RESET directive, 59
Reset Pos. (debugger), 34
Reset time option, 50
Reset timer selection, 40
RET instruction, 137, 166
RETI instruction, 138, 166
RETIW instruction, 138, 167
RETP instruction, 138, 166
Return from subroutine, 164
Return instructions, 166
RETW instruction, 138, 166
RL instruction, 139
Rotate instructions, 155
RR instruction, 139
RTCC interrupt, 99, 175
RTCC register, 153
RTCC-rollover interrupts, 100
Run - Assemble, 23
Run - Clock, 25
Run - Configure, 25
Run - Device, 25
Run - Program, 24
Run (debugger), 34
Run a program, 24
Run menu, 23

S

SASM Assembler, 43
Save file, 22
Save file as, 22
Save Hex, 41
SB instruction, 139
SC instruction, 139
Schmitt-Trigger configuration, 91
Serial port selection, 28
SETB instruction, 140
Shortcut keys (Editor), 21
SKIP instruction, 140
SLEEP instruction, 140
SLEEPCLK option, 50
SNB instruction, 140
SNC instruction, 141
SNZ instruction, 141
Software timer, 98
Software, installation of, 15
Special function registers, 153
ST_B, 169
ST_C, 171
Stack, 165
Stack overflow, 166
Stack underflow, 166
STACKX option, 48
STATUS register, 154
STC instruction, 141
Step (debugger), 34
Stop (debugger), 34
STZ instruction, 141
SUB instruction, 142
SUBB instruction, 142
Suppressing warning messages, 74
SWAP instruction, 142
SX editor, 20
SX features, 109
SX option, 48
SX pinout, 149
SX Tech Board, 145
SX-Key windows, 25
SX-Key/Blitz user interface, 19
SX-Key/Blitz, Hardware, 13
Symbolic names, 68
Symbols, 68
SYNC, 48
Syntax highlighting, 29
SZ instruction, 143

T

Tables, 103
TEST instruction, 143
Time out bit, 154
Timer/Counter interrupts, 99
Timers, multi-function, 96
TO bit, 154
Token pasting, 65
TRIS_A, 167
TRIS_B, 168
TRIS_C, 170
TTL level, 90
TURBO option, 48

U

Unary operators, 71
Undo, 22
Upgrading code to SASM, 85
User interface, 19

W

Wake up interrupts, 103
Wake up on edge detect, 93
Walk debugger, 34
Warnings, SASM, 74
Warnings, suppressing, 74
Warranty, 2
WATCH directive, 60
Watch window, 35
WATCHDOG option, 48
WDRT option, 50
Web site, 3
WKED_B, 169
WKEN_B, 169
WKPND_B, 169

X

XOR instruction, 143

Z

Z bit, 154
Zero bit, 154